ADVANCE PRAISE FOR *CALLING THE BRANDS*

"Calling the Brands *is a thorough and workmanlike look at one of the most important and romanticized parts of cattle ranching in the US. The author's look at the history of cattle branding and the rustling it is meant to contain, as well as the present-day need to continue to call the brand, is an important contribution to documenting the West that was and still is.*"
—BURT RUTHERFORD, SENIOR EDITOR, *BEEF* MAGAZINE

"Calling the Brands *is well written and an enjoyable read. Buoyed by historical facts, Monty McCord is a great storyteller of the events that helped shape today's modern cattle industry.*"
—ALLEN MOCZYGEMBA, CHIEF EXECUTIVE OFFICER,
AMERICAN ANGUS ASSOCIATION

CALLING THE BRANDS
Stock Detectives in the Wild West

MONTY McCORD

TWODOT®

GUILFORD, CONNECTICUT
HELENA, MONTANA

A · TWODOT® · BOOK

An imprint of The Rowman & Littlefield Publishing Group, Inc.
4501 Forbes Blvd., Ste. 200
Lanham, MD 20706
www.rowman.com
A registered trademark of The Rowman & Littlefield Publishing Group, Inc.

Distributed by NATIONAL BOOK NETWORK

British Library Cataloguing in Publication Information available

Library of Congress Cataloging-in-Publication Data

Names: McCord, Monty, author.
Title: Calling the brands : stock detectives in the Wild West / Monty McCord.
Description: Guilford, Connecticut : TwoDot, [2018] | Includes bibliographical references
 and index. |
Identifiers: LCCN 2017044374 (print) | LCCN 2017052773 (ebook) | ISBN 9781493030880
 (e-book) | ISBN 9781493030873 (pbk.)
Subjects: LCSH: Cattle stealing—West (U.S.)—History. | Frontier and pioneer life—West (U.S.) |
 West (U.S.)—History.
Classification: LCC HV6661.W47 (ebook) | LCC HV6661.W47 M33 2018 (print) | DDC
 363.28/9—dc23
LC record available at https://lccn.loc.gov/2017044374

∞™ The paper used in this publication meets the minimum requirements of American National
Standard for Information Sciences—Permanence of Paper for Printed Library Materials, ANSI/
NISO Z39.48-1992.

Printed in the United States of America

For Ann, who melted the hardened frame within.
And for the little wrangler, Elon.

CONTENTS

Acknowledgments

The completion of this book represents an acquired treasury of new friends and professional acquaintances without whose assistance this project would have been very difficult indeed. The life of this manuscript took many more years than originally planned, but such is the writing life. Thank you to Erin Turner of TwoDot for allowing this project to see the light of day. And thanks to dear friend and author Chris Enss for her support and encouragement. I owe a debt of gratitude to the many people mentioned here. If I manage to omit anyone, let me apologize now, for any such omission is truly unintentional.

First of all, I would like to give a very special thank you to my wife, Ann, whose untiring assistance with research and first edits and whose patience with my technology issues is so appreciated.

I would like to give thanks to Cynthia Monroe of the Nebraska State Historical Society. Mrs. Monroe was the Nebraska livestock brand recorder as part of the secretary of state's office, and then with the Nebraska Brand Committee (NBC) after 1975 when the NBC took over brand registrations. Through the years Mrs. Monroe saved two boxes full of archives covering brands and livestock enforcement in Nebraska. She was gracious and trusting enough to loan these to the author, whom she had never met before. These archives were of great value to this project; thank you.

Adam Gonzales also deserves a thank you for his assistance with research of information/photos on brand history and enforcement from New Mexico, Arizona, and Utah, and the Anti-Horse Thief Association.

My sincere thanks is also extended to Dr. Cheri Wolfe, museum and education coordinator for the Texas and Southwestern Cattle Raisers Foundation who was a pleasure to talk to and who assisted with information and photos on the Texas and Southwestern Cattle Raisers Association history.

George W. Collins generously shared information about himself and his father, Sandy, who was the first brand inspector for the state of Washington. George's own career as a state brand inspector spanned forty-six years.

I am very grateful to Chief Investigator Steven Stanec (retired) and Investigator Larry Birth (retired) of the Nebraska Brand Committee (NBC) for their cooperation in answering my many questions and supplying needed materials. Also, my thanks to Supervisory Brand Inspector Dwain Inness and Inspectors Shawn Hanks, Faron Greenbaugh, Jerry Jackson, and Jeff Fouts of the Kearney brand office of the NBC for their indulgence while I photographed and talked to them at work seventeen years ago; to Supervisory Brand Inspector Monty Sever and Inspectors Jason Gardner, Kate Zander, Ashley Berumen, and Katelyn Bennett, whom I visited and photographed as they did their inspections at the Kearney Livestock Auction in 2017; and to NBC executive director Bill Bunce for approving and arranging my visit.

My thanks go to these people and organizations: Robert Payne and Lloyd Brown, Arizona Department of Agriculture; Arizona Cattlemen's Association; Central City, Nebraska, public library; Gary Shoun (retired) and Christopher Whitney, brand commissioner, Colorado Department of Agriculture; Colorado Cattlemen's Association; Lucille White, Idaho Department of Law Enforcement, State Brand Board; Idaho State Historical Society; Carolyn Autry, Indiana Historical Society; Martha Wright, Indiana State Library; Teresa Martin, Kansas Animal Health Department; Jason Wesco, Kansas State Historical Society; Kansas Livestock Association; Merrick County (Nebraska) clerk of the District Court; Callaway, Nebraska, public library; Kearney, Nebraska, Livestock Auction; Brian Shovers, Montana Historical Society; Laura Mooney, Nebraska History Museum; Nebraska State Historical Society; Betsy Macfarlan, Nevada Cattlemen's Association; Dennis Journigan, Nevada Division of Agriculture, Bureau of Livestock Identification; James Davis, North Dakota State Historical Society; Kym Koch, Oklahoma State Bureau of Investigation; Sody Fleming, Oklahoma Department of Agriculture; Dee Cordry, Oklahombres; Oregon Cattlemen's Association; Ken Stewart, State Archives, South Dakota State Historical Society; South Dakota State Library; Connie Christensen, South Dakota Peace Officers Association; Karen Marchant, Utah Cattlemen's Association; Utah State Historical Society; Connie Monroe and Pam Potwin, Washington Department of Agriculture; Mary Marvel, Westerners International; Judy West, Wyoming State Historical Society; Kelly Hamilton, Wyoming State Brand Board; Daniel Davis and John R. Waggener, American Heritage Center, University of Wyoming; LaVaughn Bresnahan, Wyoming Division of Cultural Resources, State Archives; Tom Breen, Missouri State Highway Patrol (retired); Carolie Heyliger, National Law Enforcement Officers Memorial Fund; Steve Downie; Bob Fleming; Carl Heinrich; Rick Leaf; Sean Marschke; Paul Rogers; Chad Penn; and author Bob Alexander.

INTRODUCTION

But select capable men from all the people—men who fear God, trust worthy men who hate dishonest gain—and appoint them as officials over thousands, hundreds, fifties and tens.

—EXODUS 18:21

PEOPLE OF ALL WALKS OF LIFE AND ETHNIC ORIGIN WERE DRAWN TO the western frontier of nineteenth-century America. Many of them had religion, but some didn't. Many took pride in working hard to make a living for their families, and many just took. These predators found it much easier to take the fruit of others' toil instead of gainfully acquiring it themselves. A few of these scofflaws had been successful buffalo hunters until they decimated the great herds. It wasn't a giant leap to butchering others' cattle and spiriting away their horses.

Livestock thieves became known as "rustlers." Membership in the rustling fraternity was not only filled by ex–buffalo hunters but also cowboys, farmers, ranchers, politicians, bankers, Indians, butcher-shop owners . . . the list went on. The extent of persons involved in stealing livestock was only matched by the area they covered. By the 1870s, thefts were occurring at such high rates legitimate cattlemen had to take action themselves to save their very livelihood. Lawmen were spread thinly throughout the West and weren't able to devote the time and expense of tracking down cattle thieves. "Prairie justice," or "judge lynch's law," became the form of defense taken by the ranchers, which eliminated some rustlers, but unfortunately some innocent men were hanged in the process. It was pretty much understood that one caught on the range with livestock bearing someone else's brand meant a swift hanging, shooting, or drowning—whatever method of execution was handy.

Lynchings ensured no recidivism of the accused but did provide some amount of bad publicity for cattlemen. Some of the larger ranchers paid one of their most plucky cowhands—one who had demonstrated a proficiency with firearms—as a "protection man" for the owner's range. His orders were simple: "Eliminate the ranch's loss to rustlers." Many areas decided to organize cattlemen's associations, which operated on fees based on the number of stock owned by each member. With these proceeds, men were hired as association detectives to protect the members' ranges.

The popularity of Old West history has made many lawmen's titles familiar, such as marshal, sheriff, constable, ranger, and US marshal, to name a few. Much less familiar are the various titles used by those who protected the cattle industry from being carted away lock, stock, and barrel. This is the story of the range detectives, stock detectives, inspectors, or protection men, who often worked completely alone, courageously capturing or killing livestock rustlers in order to ensure the survivability of the industry. These men had to be proficient in reading brands to identify stock owners. These men were "calling the brands."

Many assume that the Old West era slipped away at the beginning of the new century, and with it went the cattle and horse thieves. As John Wayne once replied, "Not hardly." To provide a more complete understanding of the modern rustling problem, this volume continues its coverage to the present and introduces the reader to the state agencies and associations of the seventeen western states that are responsible for the policing of livestock interests today.

CHAPTER 1

Cowboys and Longhorns

THE CATTLE EMPIRE OF THE UNITED STATES BEGAN IN TEXAS BEFORE the Civil War. The Texas Revolution of 1836–1845 ended in favor of the victorious Texans, who took over the ranches and cattle herds north of the Rio Grande River after the Mexicans who lived there abandoned them. Cattle numbers were multiplying exponentially. The government estimated in 1830 that there were a hundred thousand head of cattle in Texas, which continued to increase at a high rate. To understand how well cattle proliferated in Texas, we need to look at the agricultural census estimates of the times. By 1850, an estimated 330,000 head existed and by 1860 the number had risen to over three million.

Because of the high number of cattle roaming the territory, the Republic of Texas announced that all unbranded cattle were public property. Ranchers went to work with branding irons, burning their brand on as many as they could handle. New ranches appeared and existing ones expanded with the additional stock.

During the 1830s, some of the first trail drives began when ranchers decided they could sell their cattle to the cities where there was a market. Between 1830 and 1856, cattle were driven to Chicago and New Orleans, as well as Arizona, New Mexico, Missouri, Ohio, and California. These drives did little to lower the number of cattle in Texas, as the herds had continued to multiply at a high rate. The Civil War put a temporary dampener on the cattle business, however. The Confederate forces were receiving Texas cattle to feed their soldiers until the Union army secured the Mississippi River, thus preventing further supply of beef to the rebels.

No figures are available for the number of cattle in Texas at the end of the war, but an 1870 census estimated five million head. After the war, cattle in Texas were worth about four dollars a head. The ranchers found that they could get forty dollars a head in the northeastern markets. To get their herds to market, they knew they would have to drive them to towns that had a railhead, such as Sedalia, Missouri, where the Missouri Pacific Railroad operated. The ranchers set out for Sedalia but soon learned that the drives through southeastern Kansas, northwestern Arkansas, and southern Missouri proved to be a perilous task, at best. Large groups of armed civilians met the cowboys with violence. Their claim was that they meant to prevent the "Texas cattle fever" from infecting their own stock, but it was often just an excuse to rob the trail herds.

Whatever the motives of the armed civilians were, the Texas or "Spanish" fever was real and caused the death of hundreds of cattle, ruining some cattlemen. The cowboys driving into this area quickly learned to avoid these routes and looked at other possibilities.

By the 1870s, there was marked progress of westerly expansion of the rail system in the United States. With a deal made by J. G. McCoy, an Illinois livestock shipper, and the Hannibal & St. Joe Railroad, reasonable shipping prices were agreed upon for the shipments between St. Joe and Chicago. After searching Kansas for the best town to accommodate a rail link to St. Joe, McCoy established one at Abilene. He built stockyards complete with loading ramps that would handle three thousand head of cattle. The cattle business quickly spread to points north as other towns such as Ellsworth, Wichita, and Dodge City, Kansas, as well as Ogallala, Nebraska, welcomed the coming railroads.

The problem of "Texas fever" was serious enough that the state of Kansas eventually enacted a law regarding Texas cattle. The law required inspections at the Indian Territory (Oklahoma)–Kansas border and had the power to hold infected cattle until fall, at the owner's expense. The US government finally acted in 1884, setting up a Bureau of Animal Industry, which had the power to regulate cattle traffic and suppress bovine diseases. Many states joined in the regulation and disease control of livestock in the nineteenth century. Cattle sanitary boards and bureaus of animal industry were created for these purposes. For example, in Nebraska, the

Livestock Sanitary Board was created by an act on March 5, 1885. This act provided for a Livestock Sanitary Commission of three members and a state veterinary surgeon, all appointed by the governor. The legislature of 1901 repealed existing legislation and made the governor the state veterinarian, with power to appoint a deputy for the actual work of the post. In 1913, the Nebraska legislature again repealed the act and created a Livestock Sanitary Board of five members, still appointed by the governor, who continued with the title of "state veterinarian." The legislature of 1919 repealed laws of 1913 as pertaining to the establishment of the Livestock Sanitary Board, and established the Bureau of Animal Industry as part of the new Department of Agriculture, with the state veterinarian in charge. The Nebraska Bureau of Animal Industry was charged with the supervision of the regulation and movement of livestock into Nebraska, and handling of domestic animals within the state where infectious, contagious, and otherwise transmittable diseases occur. The bureau cooperated with the US Bureau of Animal Industry in certain specific diseases affecting livestock.

The Texans, among many others, discovered the seemingly endless sea of grass on the central and western Great Plains region of the country. Virtually everything west of the Mississippi River was government-owned land. The Texas cattlemen, as well as wealthy Easterners and foreign immigrants, established ranches in the Dakotas, Wyoming, Nebraska, Montana, Colorado, New Mexico, and Arizona. Many of the immigrants came from Ireland, Scotland, England, France, and Germany. The majority of these outside investors essentially operated the ranches by proxy. They would hire a dependable ranch foreman who managed the ranch year-round and make an appearance at the spring and fall round-ups. They would keep their homes in the East or in San Francisco in the West, or join the growing society of cattlemen in Cheyenne. To many, the cattle ranch was a business and not a home.

The cowboys who were hired to work the ranches brought with them the usual personal accoutrements, such as their horses, lariats, and in some cases, a six-shooter. Not being "heeled" (armed) while working wasn't uncommon for many cowboys. However, carrying a six-shooter was necessary under some circumstances, such as when working in hostile Indian territories or with the expectation of an attack by a personal antagonist (which obviously wasn't always foreseeable), encountering trespassers and/or rustlers on the range, for animals that presented a danger to livestock, for killing sick or injured cattle, when visiting ranches or towns, and when calling on a woman. Yes, the six-gun even served as a part of being fully dressed for formal occasions, which included impressing the targeted female.

The attacks by rustlers became so flagrant in 1869 that Williamson County, Texas, cattleman Isom Prentice Olive ordered all of his cowboys to carry a six-shooter on their hip and keep a repeating rifle on their saddle. From that point on, the Olive crew was called a "gun outfit." Fellow rancher John Shaw endorsed Olive's order when he told a friend, "A man's got a right to protect himself, and in this cow business he needs a gun to do it!"

In a period of ten to fifteen years, the cattle business expanded from Mexico and Texas to the establishment of ranches all over the West. The ranchers, with their cattle and horses, held possession of the unclaimed land by proprietary rights for several years to come. They held "range rights," which gave them the right to build on, live on, raise their stock on, and furthermore, regulate their stated boundaries. Established near water and good grass, the ranchers actually held no legal government title to the land they occupied. As the country continued its westward expansion, these "range rights" would be put to a bitter test.

As more and more new ranchers settled in with their small herds, undoubtedly hoping for future expansion and success, they soon learned that no matter where they established their ranches, it seemed to be on someone else's spread. Unfortunately, some of the early ranchers claimed up to ten thousand square miles as "their range"!

In 1862, the Homestead Act was passed by Congress. This act provided that any person over twenty-one years of age, who was head of the family, and a citizen or an alien who intended to become a citizen, could easily obtain title to 160 acres of public land. The homesteader was required to live on the land for at least five years and to improve it (e.g., build a living structure or dig a well). Between 1862 and 1900, this offer of free land to settlers brought over half a million families west. These people were or became farmers who turned the soil and grass to plant crops, with varying degrees of success. It didn't rain often on the western plains and most of the creeks and rivers had already been claimed by ranchers. Disputes fired up between the two groups fighting for the rights to water as well as the land.

By the early 1870s the cattle business had become a relatively successful venture. That would come to an abrupt halt in 1873 when corn crops in Texas failed, the northern ranges couldn't handle any more cattle, and the market demand had seriously weakened. In September of 1873 the New York bank Jay Cooke & Company closed, which started the first panic that the cattle business ever knew. A shipping firm lost $180,000 in a matter of a few weeks. One cattleman shipped his stock to Chicago to sell but failed to make enough to pay the freight expenses. After the panic of 1873, trail drives diminished due to the saturated ranges. Packing plants were built in Chicago, St. Louis, and Kansas City, at which time cattle production decreased in the East, making the industry more dependent on beef from the West.

As the 1880s approached, the cattle industry was in an upward swing, realizing profits once again. Well-fed northern range cattle were bringing sixty dollars a head and a Texas steer about forty to fifty dollars. Various influences fueled the boom. Many railroads crossed the plains, establishing towns and bringing all the new settlers they could carry. The railroads hoped for future income from these newly established towns. Money seemed to be plentiful in the entire country, which made a good time for investing in business ventures. Another contributing factor was the final containment of the Indians, who were by then residing mostly on government reservations. A race to the free land of the West began, with farmers and ranchers staking out even more land before it was too late.

By 1882, the boom was at its height, with ranchers making up to 300 percent profit on cattle purchased three years earlier. A large demand for beef reduced the number of cattle on the previously overstocked ranges, which made prices rise. The overused ranges soon became worn out, with little or no grass left by 1883 when the country was hit by a drought. Texas was affected much worse than other areas, with one ranch reporting that over the winter they lost fifteen thousand out of their herd of twenty-five thousand cattle.

Prices again started to decline by 1884, and by the following year prices crashed. If they sold at all, range cattle previously worth thirty to thirty-five dollars a head now brought less than ten dollars. The rest of the century was a very hard time for cattlemen. In 1887, the highest quality steers brought $2.40 per hundred pounds at the Chicago market. The rancher could make a profit of about eight dollars on a 1,200-pound steer. The handwriting was on the wall. The rancher realized that if he could hang on, the cattle business would be changing. Farmers were streaming into range country to ply their trade using the new barbed wire to protect their homesteads. The "free ranges" were being fenced by many ranchers who wanted to be sure that they had enough land to support their herds. Due to the gradual loss of the open range, the type of cattle raised would no longer be steers raised on free grass. Food and water would have to be provided to the stock in different ways. If the cattleman no longer had access to water, he had to drill wells equipped with windmills. The cowboys would have to add the job of repairing windmills to their list of duties, along with fence mending.

CHAPTER 2

Rope 'em and Brand 'em

THE AGE AND ORIGIN OF THE BRAND MAY BE SURPRISING TO SOME. IT IS easy to imagine the livestock brand having its beginnings on the cattle ranches of Texas, where the cattle industry began. However, the brand is something Americans cannot lay claim to as an original. The exact origin of brands is unknown, but we can trace them back to 2000 BC when Egyptian writings indicated that the pharaohs branded their cattle as well as their slaves. The Greeks and Romans also utilized branding as a means to identify the position one held, including that of a criminal. The latest record of human branding is about 1830, involving French slaves.

In 1521, Spaniard Gregorio de Villalobos brought a small herd of Andalusian cattle to what is now Mexico, where he established the first cattle ranch in North America. Two years earlier, Don Hernán Cortés had invaded New Spain (Mexico) and conquered the Aztecs. Cortés took many captives, who were then branded on the cheek with a "G" for *guerra* (war) and sold into slavery. While Cortés was obsessed with hunting for treasure, Villalobos prospered with his growing cattle herd. Later Cortés would follow suit and start his own cattle ranch. He is credited with being the first to brand cattle in North America, using three Christian crosses for his brand.

In 1529 the Mexico City town council organized the first cattlemen's organization, the Mesta. The council ordered that the cattlemen would meet in Mexico City twice a year for reporting strays in their herds and possibly finding the rightful owners. The council also directed the cattlemen to design their own brand, like no other, and register that brand in what is known as the first brand book, which was kept in Mexico City. In time, the use of brand books would spread all over the American West.

As soon as the Spanish cattlemen started to use open grazing lands, thieves went to work. Their makeup resembled that of the rustlers of the Old West. They were people who made their living by stealing and selling livestock, and the poor who killed cattle to feed their starving families. In response to pleas from cattlemen, the government expanded the Mesta throughout all of New Spain. Added to the law were guidelines for the use of brands, earmarks, and settling of disputes over duplicate brands. The law included the policing and punishment of livestock thieves.

The use of the brand had obviously spread over the years, as evidenced by an advertisement in a Philadelphia newspaper in 1765 that asked for the return of a "brown mare pony, branded K on the left shoulder, last seen on the north edge of town."

Before the independence of Texas in 1836, Stephen Austin submitted a code of civil and criminal law for approval of the Mexican government.

Branding time on a western Nebraska ranch, ca. 1890s. COURTESY NEBRASKA BRAND COMMITTEE

Included in the document were two laws, one requiring the registration of cattle brands and the other for the disposition of estrays.

In the 1860s Texas law required cattlemen who were herding their livestock north to burn a "trail brand" on the left side behind the shoulder, so any strays picked up during the drive could more easily be cut out. It would also be easier to prove ownership of those strays. Northbound herds often included cattle from multiple ranches, who paid the main outfit to drive their cattle north.

The maverick laws of the West, which related to the ownership of cattle found on the open prairie without a brand, would become important. The term "maverick" originated from a signer of the Texas Declaration of Independence, Samuel Augustus Maverick. In 1845 Maverick accepted around four hundred head of cattle to settle a neighbor's debt. Having much stronger interests in other areas, he neglected to brand the calves that were produced. Cowboys riding for Shanghai Pierce, as well as others, generally called these unbranded cattle "Maverick's." This term became so widely accepted that it has since been used to identify any unbranded cattle on the open range.

Steamboat captain Richard King purchased a Mexican land grant in south Texas in 1853. Profits from partnering with Mifflin Kenedy in a successful steamboat company opened the door for the two men to establish a ranch. In 1859, King registered his first brand, which was the "HK connected," in honor of his wife, Henrietta. Later the same year King registered the "R Arrow." Kenedy and King split their ranch holdings in 1868, and the now famous "Running W" brand used by King in the 1860s was registered in 1869. Kenedy and King set to work expanding their own famous ranches. Today, the lands that make up the legendary King Ranch encompass 825,000 acres.

Webster's *New World Dictionary* defines pyrography as "the art or process of burning designs on wood or leather by the use of heated tools." John Hale, an expert collector and historian of branding irons, coined the phrase "American pyroglyphics." It means a combination of plane geometry, the alphabet, and Arabic numerals that are used together to comprise the branding alphabet. The main purpose of a brand is not only to establish a mark of ownership but also to mark the critter so the brand cannot be easily changed by thieves. It was not uncommon for early cowboys to be unable to read printing or writing, but they could easily read and memorize livestock brands. This was particularly true of the stock detectives and inspectors whose job it was to settle ownership disputes by peaceful or other means.

Ranches were usually many miles apart and with no restrictive fences, cattle intermingled and grazed together. The brands the cattle wore would help identify them and allow them to be returned to the proper owner. The cowboys would gladly cut out the strays with his neighbor's brand and head them back toward their home range. This was the hospitable thing to do and it was a benefit to all ranchers. It was part of the "code of the West."

The 1974 *Kansas Brand Laws and Regulations* handbook outlined helpful tips on branding:

> —*Proper heat of an iron is the color of ashes. A red-hot iron starts hair on fire, and usually results in a poor brand.*
> —*Use of small irons result in unreadable brands. Thin, burned up irons will cut too deeply, or make a thin scar which covers over by hair.*
> —*The Brand Law doesn't specify brand size, but each character or symbol should be 3½ or 4 inches at the highest and widest points and the face of the brand should be at least ¼ inch wide.*
> —*Use a separate iron for each character in your brand, as two or more letters or characters joined together will not heat or burn evenly, resulting in an unreadable brand.*
> —*Don't brand wet or damp animals, as the brand will scald and leave a blotch, a bad sore, or no brand at all.*
> —*The hair should be clipped before hot iron is applied. The iron should burn deeply enough to remove hair and the outer layer of skin. When iron is removed, the brand should be the color of saddle leather.*

Freeze branding is an alternative to the hot iron brand. Developed by Dr. Keith Farrell of Pullman, Washington, freeze branding was first used in Sweden in the 1960s. Some prefer the resulting white brand, which shows up better at a distance.

There is a proper technique for reading livestock brands; they are always read from left to right, top to bottom, and outside to inside.

Numbers/Symbols
—in a horizontal position are called "lazy"
—in a slanting position are called "tumbling"
—with little wings are called "flying"
—which are square or rectangular are called a "box"
—with a rocker underneath are called "rocking"
—when suspended are called "swinging"
—when a diagonal line are called a "slash"
—when a large O are called a "circle"
—when a wide O are a "mashed O" or "goose egg"
—a long horizontal line are called a "rail"
—two horizontal lines are called "two rails"
— three horizontal lines are called a "stripe"
—a short horizontal line are called a "bar"

The state of Nebraska formalized the use of brands with "An act relating to the use of marks and brands on livestock," of the Laws of Nebraska, which took effect June 1, 1879; however, it is known that the marking and branding of livestock in Nebraska did occur before that date. According to chapter 51 of Marks and Brands, Laws of Nebraska (1891 edition):

*SECTION 1. [**Record**] Every person having cattle, hogs and sheep shall have a mark or brand, different from the mark or brand of his neighbors, and he shall deliver to the county clerk a description of his mark or brand, and such clerk shall record the same in a well bound book kept by him for that purpose.*

The law dictated that no two persons were supposed to have or adopt the same mark or brand, or record the same mark or brand. When hogs or sheep were over six months old, and cattle over twelve months old, they were to be marked or branded. If any dispute arose about the question of whose mark or brand it was, it would be settled by the records of the county clerk. Section 5 laid out the penalty for using the brand of another, stating that anyone having a mark that was already recorded to someone else would be fined from twenty to a thousand dollars. To compel the honesty and accuracy of brand recording by county clerks, the law covered the liability they had if errors were made: "If any county clerk shall record the same mark or brand to more than one person, he shall forfeit and pay, to the use of the county, a fine not exceeding one hundred dollars." Additional provisions laid out a one-hundred-dollar fine for anyone willfully altering or misbranding other's stock, which showed that offenses of this type were looked at much more seriously on the range where a lynching might occur than they were in the state capitol where laws were enacted.

On February 14, 1857, Ambrose Shelly recorded the first mark in Richardson County, Nebraska, which was a crop off the right ear and a slit off the left ear. A mark and a brand were recorded on page 1 of the brand record book by the Fillmore County clerk on April 21, 1879, a month and a half before the law went into effect. F. L. Smith registered "a round hole in left ear," and C. A. Weirner registered the "Circle W on right hip." Even though a good start, the laws at this time did nothing to prevent the same brand being used in different counties. To illustrate how difficult a job it would have been to keep marks and brands straight, here is how the rest of page 1 from Fillmore County reads:

C.C. Miles	–M– on right shoulder	Apr. 30, 1880
J.B. Thompson	Round hole in both ears	Apr. 24, 1880
J.E. Spron	Round hole in right ear	Dec. 1, 1880
J.H. Ward	W on left shoulder	Apr. 30, 1881
Saml Rhirekasst	Swallow fork in left ear	Aug. 16, 1881
R.B. Campbell	C on left shoulder	Apr. 28, 1883
F.H. Briggs	B on left shoulder	Apr. 28, 1883
C.A. Smith	Crop off left ear	Apr. 28, 1883
W.O. Huffman	Figure 7 on right hip	May 28, 1883
Jacob Weis	W on right shoulder	Apr. 1, 1884
John A. Deupstin	D on right hip	Oct. 29, 1885
William Bell	Figure "5" on left hip	Mch. 24, 1887

Henry Frewert	*Swallow fork in right ear,*	
	and slit in left	*Oct. 15, 1889*
Watson Weldon	*Crop off right ear*	*Feb. 16, 1899*

Records from the county clerk of Webster County, Nebraska, indicated these registrations:

"I claim for my brand Circle P on left shoulder of horses & mules."

James D. Post
Filed May 28, 1888

"This is to certify that I have taken the letters H.D. on any part of animal, for my brand. Cattle to be run in Webster Co. Nebr."

Z. W. Moon
Filed April 8, 1886

"Red Cloud Nebr. April 23, 1889, This is to certify that I have adopted the figure 6 to be used on left hip from branding cattle and claim the same for my own brand."

Edwin E. Burr

The evolution of brand laws rightfully continued. A new act took effect in Nebraska on July 1, 1899, that created a state registry of marks and brands as well as a state mark and brand committee, and provided for marks and brands on livestock. It indicated that the governor would appoint three reputable stock raisers who were residents of the state and were "men of judgment and experience in marks and brands" to hold two-year terms. The said three appointees, together with the secretary of state, constituted the state brand and mark committee.

Any person who wanted to use a brand or mark was required to file a brand certificate with the Nebraska secretary of state for a fee of $1.50, which monies paid for the operation of the committee and expenses that the secretary of state incurred. Brands and marks were to be filed with the secretary of state on or before December 31, 1899. The committee was to meet with the secretary of state on the first Monday of January

Chute branding in Idaho, ca. 1900. COURTESY IDAHO STATE HISTORICAL SOCIETY

1900, where all brand certificates would be examined for duplicates and conflicts. The secretary would then notify owners of conflicting brands that continued use would be illegal.

A stiffer penalty awaited those who violated the new law. Any person who violated or failed to obey the provisions of the act, or continued to use a brand or mark after it had been rejected by the brand committee, was in violation. Anyone who continued to use any brands or marks after the brand committee ruled that they conflicted with a previously recorded brand or mark was deemed guilty of misdemeanor. The penalty after being convicted in court was a fine not exceeding one thousand dollars or by imprisonment in the county jail for a term not exceeding one year, or both such fine and imprisonment.

Apparently S. E. Starrett, a clerk in Secretary of State W. F. Porter's office, spent the night in the old state capitol building on the night of June 30–July 1, 1899. At around 3:30 a.m., rancher Charles T. Stewart filed an application for a brand, the very first state of Nebraska registered brand. Stewart was the secretary of the Milldale Farm and Livestock Improvement Co., an Iowa corporation that had owned ranches in Nebraska since 1883. That famous first brand was the "7HL connected."

The first brand law in South Dakota was a Dakota territorial law enacted in 1862. Brands were required to be filed with the registrar of deeds in each county. The earliest recorded brand in the Dakota Territory was that of Charles Brazzo, of Union County, on February 16, 1865.

In 1864 the first Montana Territorial Assembly at Bannack passed "An act concerning marks and brands," which was a small first step in establishing a brand recording system. The act was lacking, however, any means to enforce range and livestock protection laws. At the thirteenth legislative assembly in Helena in 1883, Chouteau County representative Joseph A. Baker introduced a bill, "An act for the better protection of the stock interests of Montana Territory." Unfortunately, the bill wasn't well written and Governor Crosby vetoed it. During the same year, stock association members, frustrated with the continued theft of their livestock, decided to hire a stock detective in each county to track down rustlers. As these detectives were not law officers, they could only present their evidence to officials and hope action would be taken. It seemed that this method wasn't particularly effective, because in 1884 a different plan was undertaken by unknown riders who grabbed up rustlers and prompted hanged them.

The legislature of 1885 took positive action by establishing the Montana Board of Stock Commissioners, which was made up of six commissioners appointed by the governor. This board was given the authority to hire stock inspectors and detectives to enforce the territorial livestock laws. Brand and mark recording had been the responsibility of county clerks, the state supreme court clerk, and the territorial treasurers until 1887, when the job was turned over to the Board of Stock Commissioners. The board then carried out the inspection, law enforcement, and brand recording duties of the territory, and state, after Montana was admitted to the union in 1889.

CHAPTER 3

Brand Burners, Slow Elk, and John Law

THE TERM "RUSTLER" WAS FIRST RECORDED ABOUT 1820. THE TERM went through a progression of meanings in the West until 1882, when it was first used in newsprint to refer to those who "rushed and hustled" cattle or horses off the range by stealing them.

Rustlers used various ploys to make off with other people's cattle. Some thieves used a "running iron," which is a simple branding iron that had either a straight or L-shaped end. These types of irons made it easy to mark over an existing brand, changing its design. The running irons were also used to draw a desired brand on unbranded mavericks. If the rustler didn't have a running iron, he would remove the cinch ring from his saddle and hold it over a fire by using two sticks.

Brand "blotting" was another technique used by the arrant thief when a brand was found that would be difficult to change. The legitimate brand was simply blotted out so it was impossible to decipher. Then it was the rustler's word against the owner as to who the cow belonged to. In a case like this, a stock detective would insist that the cow be slaughtered so he could inspect the backside of the hide, where the original brand was most evident.

The name "rustler" was attached to many men in the West, whether true or not. A rustler might have been any newcomer to the area where large ranch concerns were already established. A man and his family often had the desire to start their own ranch with a few head of cattle that they brought with them, or after they had bought a few head once settled. The large rancher, not wanting an encroaching cattle operation started near him, nor sod turned, would hinder the newcomer's progress at every chance, from damming up the source for water to preventing the settler from running cattle on *his* range. The big rancher wanted no part of contributing to the nester's herd during the night—at least that's what was sometimes thought. When all else failed, he was not above making outright threats to convince the newcomers to relocate elsewhere. They often did just that. In Dan Cushman's book *The Great North Trail*, he made the observation that "fully half of the rustlers hanged during the early days of the West were homesteaders trying to get started in the cattle business."

There was also a large number of rustlers who were really true to their name. This group actually represented the many outlaws who made their living stealing cattle. They would steal enough to build a sizable herd and then drive them to a market that wasn't particular about a mixture of brands or how legible they were. Sometimes a "range entrepreneur"

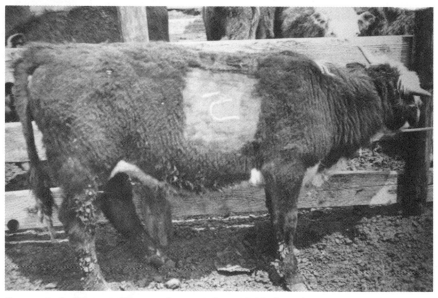

Removal of winter growth reveals an easily readable brand. COURTESY NEBRASKA BRAND COMMITTEE

would butcher a cow out on the range and dispose of the hide that held the brand. Getting caught in this act ensured the rustler of a necktie party without further ado. One such occasion occurred in Custer County, Nebraska, in 1878.

The Olive brothers moved their ranching business from Texas to Nebraska, in part to get away from the continual, deadly fights with rustlers in Williamson County, one of which cost them the life of a brother. The fact that Bob Olive was wanted by the Texas Rangers also contributed to the decision to move. The eldest brother, Isom Prentice "Print" Olive, was the boss. They found beautiful range lands in west-central Nebraska, where their herds flourished. They soon found the state had rustlers too. Bob Olive, who went by the alias Bob Stevens after arriving in Nebraska, had the duty to keep an eye out for thieves. He found out about two possible candidates. Luther Mitchell, his wife and children, and Ami Ketchum had homesteaded in the area and shared a large sod house. Rumors of their thefts were not uncommon. Visitors to their homestead were fed, in the true spirit of western hospitality. When asked about the delicious meat served, Ketchum would offer a sly smile and tell them it was "slow elk," which was a colloquialism for stolen beef. Their day in the sun would turn cloudy when "Stevens" found Olive-branded cattle at the market in Kearney Junction. Giving proof to Buffalo County sheriff Dave Anderson, he was deputized to arrest Ami Ketchum. Taking a couple of Olive cowboys with him, he announced upon arrival at the homestead that Ketchum was under arrest. Gunfire was the response, one bullet finding "Stevens." The posse escaped to a nearby homestead, where Bob "Stevens" Olive died. This was a serious mistake on the part of Ketchum and Mitchell, as Print was very close to his younger brother.

Sheriffs in nearby counties tracked down the two homesteaders, who had fled eastward, and arrested them for the murder. They were transferred by train to Plum Creek, where Keith County sheriff Barney Gillan and Custer County deputy sheriff Phil DuFran were to transport the prisoners by wagon to the court of jurisdiction in Custer County. Midway through their trip one night, the wagon was stopped by Print Olive and several of his cowboys. Print had posted a $750 reward and "offered" it to the two lawmen in exchange for the prisoners. The trade was made.

With ropes around their necks, standing in the wagon, Print shot Mitchell and hung both men. Shortly afterward, both bodies were burned by parties unknown, while still hanging from the tree branch. Rightfully or not, Print Olive earned the sobriquet "the Nebraska man-burner."

Olive and his cowboys were arrested, but only Print and his foreman, Fred Fisher, stood trial. They were convicted and sent to the Nebraska state prison in Lincoln. After spending nineteen months behind bars, Olive's attorneys were successful in winning a new trial. Because William Gaslin, the original judge, chose not hold the trial in the county where the lynching took place, the state supreme court ordered a new trial to be held in the proper jurisdiction. No witnesses appeared to testify against Olive or Fisher at the second trial and the charges were dismissed.

Retired Special Texas Ranger Augustus Judson Votaw, conveys the tough countenance of an old-time livestock inspector.
COURTESY TEXAS CATTLE RAISERS MUSEUM

Innocent mistakes were made too. For instance, in 1901, a seventeen-year-old boy was arrested by Montana stock inspector Dake upon complaint of a Mr. Moses. It seemed that Mr. Ailing engaged the boy to round up some of his horses from the range. Payment for the work would be a certain colt running with an MK branded mare. The work was completed, but by mistake, the boy ran in a mare and colt owned by Mr. Moses, the complainant. The newspaper commented, "Mr. Moses, unlike his biblical namesake, was neither tongue-tied nor slow to wrath. Hence the arrest of the boy." It was an easy mistake to make, the mare *was* branded with an MK—but on the opposite side than where Mr.

Ailing's horses were branded. The error was explained to the justice of the peace and the boy was released.

Along with local auction sales, town butcher shops would become a regular stop for livestock inspectors. They would examine the brands on hides as well as corresponding bills of sale. At times, those who had anything to do with cattle were considered rustlers but upon close examination it was difficult to tell. That is not to say, however, that reputable ranchers sometimes wouldn't cut out a steer for a struggling family of settlers to butcher, especially if they had children.

The frustration experienced by local lawmen contending with rustlers was far reaching. One such case played out in northern Nebraska. The mouth of the Niobrara River is located on the northern border of Knox County, Nebraska. The county seat was established there in 1877 and was named after the river. Sam and Jim Rothwell moved to Creighton, in the southern part of the county, and built a ranch with an ever-expanding cattle herd. They started a new ranch on the Santee Indian Reservation, when settlers were allowed to live there. It was said that on cattle drives they would "pick up" large numbers of extras from other herds that happened to mingle into the Rothwells' herds. Only if the owner of the stray cattle made a fuss would he be allowed to cut out his livestock. Otherwise, the whole mixed herd went to market and the large sums collected went into the Rothwells' pockets.

In 1890, Sam Rothwell got into a dispute with Charles Crocket over the latter's farm. During the quarrel Rothwell shot Crocket, who later recovered from the wound. Rothwell was never charged with the deadly assault, presumably because of the level of power the brothers had reached by this time with their stolen cattle operations. In a peculiar turn of events, Charles Crocket was elected Knox County sheriff the following year.

The Rothwells' operation became more brazen as time went by, with entire herds going missing. They were suspected of the thefts, but even more surely, of the disposition of the cattle. During August of 1893 the Rothwells slipped up by getting caught loading a Mr. Nelson's cattle on a train. They said they bought them from George Thomas, a relative of Nelson. The two Rothwells and Thomas were arrested and placed in the county jail at Niobrara. Apparently they had been shipping stolen cattle to Omaha where Link, a third Rothwell brother, lived.

Soon the area was visited by other area lawmen looking for cattle stolen from their jurisdictions. The Holt County sheriff was looking for a herd of around two hundred cattle. Link arrived to help the brothers, just in time to be arrested by the Pierce County sheriff and jailed at Pierce. Five other rustlers were arrested and lodged at Niobrara, nearly filling the county jail to capacity. Omaha newspapers reported that a number of "prominent citizens" were under arrest for cattle rustling in Knox County. The people of that county were tired of the large-scale thieving that had been going on. Talk soon moved around to the subject of lynching the entire bunch. Sheriff Crocket easily caught wind of the dangerous mood in town and deputized fifty men, all armed with Winchester rifles, to guard the jail. One of Jim Rothwell's friends tried to smuggle a revolver to him, but it was intercepted by the vigilant sheriff.

A large crowd formed around the jail, demanding that the prisoners be sent out. They were prepared to hang them all and put a stop to the area's rustling problems. Sheriff Crocket and his deputies, armed to the teeth, refused their commands. Finally, after several hours, the crowd thinned out when they realized it would cost some of their own lives to have the privilege of hanging the rotten bunch. Crocket was respected by the citizens, even though they thought the prisoners should hang. A comment in the fiery town newspaper illustrated the sour mood of the people: "Nobody gets lynched in this country but some friendless nigger because the American people are too cowardly to hang a man with money and friends."

One of the prisoners testified against the Rothwells and they were all bound over to district court. The Rothwells hired the best attorneys money could buy, and they were successful in winning a change of venue to Neligh, in Antelope County. The trial, bitterly fought by both sides, failed to convict the rustlers. Sheriff Crocket must have shaken his head in disgust as he witnessed his prisoners saunter out of the courtroom.

On occasion, in spite of lawfully detaining suspected rustlers, the outrage of the public took over. A number of horses had been stolen from Sam Dedrick in New Mexico. A posse was organized and began tracking the herd. When they came upon the rustlers, a gunfight broke out, which resulted in the death of the gang leader. The two other rustlers were taken to Kelly, in Socorro County, New Mexico, where they were confined inside a house. That night, a number of masked men surrounded the house and took the prisoners away from the posse. They found a tree, hanged the two, and shot them full of holes. A news account explained that "The men lynched were Mexicans and desperate."

Newspapers often ran stories that were captioned "Rustler Strung Up" or some such, but in July 1895, another incident that occurred in northern Nebraska was reported with the heading "RUSTLERS NOT HANGED." The *Santa Fe Daily New Mexican* reported that it took a group of fifteen vigilantes ten days to capture a gang of four rustlers. The thieves denied their crimes, until they were led under a cottonwood tree where lariats were prepared. The four admitted what they'd done with hopes that the admission would prevent their hanging. It did. They were jailed in Springview, Nebraska, to await trial. The newspaper noted, "The only wonder is that the rustlers were not hung or shot on sight, as about half of the committee after them were old time vigilantes." The paper also said that the people were up in arms and new vigilante committees had been formed with the intention that, from then on, cattle rustlers *would be hanged*.

Park County, Wyoming, sheriff Rice Hutsenpillar faced an unusual situation where his rustler-prisoner didn't make it to court. After the sheriff had arrested the man and bail was paid, he was released pending trial. On the day of the trial, Sheriff Hutsenpillar went to the accused man's room to get him and found that he had been drinking as usual. When they walked out of the room to the stairs, the inebriated man tripped and fell down the entire flight of stairs. As he fell, he bit off a large chunk of his tongue and bled to death before help could arrive.

Territorial (and later county) sheriffs were the lawmen who commonly received ranchers' complaints of stock theft. Although their primary duties were to enforce the law, preserve the peace, maintain the county jail, serve court processes, and collect taxes, sheriffs were also active in the fight against rustling. In addition, sometimes other livestock-oriented duties were added to their responsibilities. A proclamation issued on March 25,

1904, by Nebraska governor John Mickey stated, "All cattle should be dipped when disease is known to exist . . . the sheriffs of the counties are instructed to see that the proclamation is enforced."

Tracking down rustlers created difficulties for county sheriffs. The job took a lot of time, from several days to weeks or more, while their other duties were neglected. Those that elected the sheriff didn't care for him to be gone for long periods either. Oftentimes the county couldn't afford the expenses that a long chase would incur and the rustlers knew this. It could be a dangerous job as well. Rustlers would sometimes resort to violence to avoid the cold iron bars. The sheriffs did the best they could with the available resources.

Sheriffs were often assisted with livestock cases by range detectives who were employed by a ranch owner for the sole purpose of stopping rustlers. These detectives had the time, patience, and sometimes the requisite funding for tracking down thieves. E. C. "Teddy Blue" Abbott said in his book, *We Pointed Them North*, "The rustlers of that day were a different class of men from the sneak thieves of today. . . . They went in armed bands, took what they wanted by force, and defied arrest. It came to a showdown, fight or quit." The rustling problem wouldn't go away, and many ranchers would be in financial trouble if something wasn't done. The next logical step for them was to organize.

CHAPTER 4

The Cattlemen's Associations

THE CONTINUOUS THEFT OF LIVESTOCK, THE LOW RATE OF CONVICTION of those caught, and poor legislative support led the cattlemen to band together. The cowman had never been accused of being a joiner, but times were tough and there seemed to be no other choice. In fact, it made sense. A solid organization of many cattlemen would have a voice that could be heard in Washington, on the territorial or state level, and if necessary, on the range. The ranchers were in such a perilous state of affairs that they considered this a time of life or death for their business and their very welfare.

THE ARIZONA CATTLEMEN'S ASSOCIATION

In 1904, a small group of cattlemen organized the Arizona Cattle Growers Association (ACGA). These founding members were primarily concerned with having orderly, systematic laws in place that would protect livestock and property. The ACGA was incorporated in 1924.

In 1934, the Arizona Cattle Feeders Association (ACFA) was organized and incorporated, which makes it the oldest feeder organization in the United States.

The Arizona Cattlemen's Association (ACA) was established in 1986, which streamlined the administrative functions of the ACGA and ACFA. Both groups have maintained their individual directors and identities. The organizations represent over forty thousand beef cattle producers in the state. US Department of Agriculture statistics for 1996 indicated that there were over eight hundred thousand head of cattle in Arizona.

THE CALIFORNIA CATTLEMEN'S ASSOCIATION

By the turn of the twentieth century, cattlemen had organized the California Stockraisers Association (CSA). In 1901, the CSA announced the founding of another association called the Southwestern Stockmen, with seventy-three charter members that included the wealthiest and most prominent stockmen of central California. Purposes set forth were to stress enforcement of quarantine laws as well as the protection of herds from all contagious diseases and from the raids of the rustlers and thieves. Rewards were offered for the arrest and conviction of rustlers, and the association had posses "available night and day to take the trail."

The California Cattlemen's Association (CCA) was established in 1917 and is headquartered in Sacramento. The association was formed to represent the state's cattle industry in legislative and regulatory affairs. The CCA is an affiliate of the National Cattlemen's Beef Association, with offices in Denver, Chicago, and Washington, DC. The CCA includes thirty-eight county cattlemen's associations, which makes it a strong entity.

Another organization was formed in 1925, the California Cattlemen's Cooperative Association. It served members in Arizona, Nevada, southern Oregon, and southwestern New Mexico.

THE COLORADO CATTLEMEN'S ASSOCIATION

In the 1860s, four Colorado counties—Fremont, Boulder, Arapahoe, and El Paso—formed what they called the Colorado Cattle Association. Their purpose was to prevent herds of Texas cattle from being driven near settlements, as they were a danger to their "American" cattle. If the members had to, they would apply to authorities to enforce the law that forbade the importation of Texas cattle for any purpose.

The cattlemen formally organized the Colorado Cattlemen's Association in 1867. At their annual convention five years later in Denver, the association invited stock growers from neighboring territories, as they felt common goals were worth exploring. Sixteen Wyoming stockmen attended this convention, five of whom were charter members of the Wyoming Stock Graziers Association, which had been formed in Laramie in 1871. The topics discussed at this convention were the planned management of roundups, the repression of livestock theft, and the regulation of brands.

The association went through several name changes over the years, mainly to stay in touch with changes in policies, politics, and economics.

THE IDAHO CATTLE ASSOCIATION

In 1915, the Idaho Cattle and Horse Growers Association (ICHGA) was formed. In 1983, the ICHGA and the Idaho Cattle Feeders Association merged to become the Idaho Cattle Association (ICA). In the late 1990s, the Idaho CattleWomen, Inc. merged with the ICA.

The association has over one thousand members and represents over six thousand cattle-producing families for a total of almost two million head of cattle. The mission of the ICA is to coordinate and advance the economic well-being of the Idaho beef industry through innovative and effective political, educational, and marketing programs accepted and supported by all industry segments, partners, and coalitions.

THE KANSAS LIVESTOCK ASSOCIATION

In 1883 the first two livestock associations were formed in Kansas. In February the farmers and ranchers in the eastern part of the state established the Shorthorn Breeders Association of Kansas. The first meeting was held in Topeka, the state capitol. The Western Kansas Cattle Growers Association (WKCGA) was formed in April of the same year during a meeting of stockmen in Dodge City. This organization was obviously meant for the large cattlemen and ranch owners as the cost to join was fifteen dollars, with annual dues of ten dollars. To put this into perspective, the cowboy generally earned one dollar per day, or thirty dollars a month.

The WKCGA members were instructed that they were not to let any unknown or suspicious persons on their ranges or ranches. This went against the frontier custom of offering complete hospitality to visitors.

Another resolution that the association passed was "to prevent the carrying of firearms by cattlemen at all times and places except when absolutely necessary." The association believed that carrying firearms led to evildoing and was dangerous to people and property. No doubt many cowboys laughed at this, but some probably did follow the rules. The average cowboy wasn't a gunfighter by any stretch of the imagination, as he carried a six-shooter for protection from varmints of all types. Cowboys had enough sense to unbuckle the shooter when climbing aboard a bronc, because landing on three pounds of iron between you and the ground could cause serious injury.

Additionally, the members were not to brand mavericks until the end of the spring roundup. Nonmembers were more or less shunned and were not to be helped with their cattle in any way. They also addressed the cattle theft problem by posting a $500 reward for conviction of rustlers and called for the publication of a brand book. Records indicate that the WKCGA met again in 1884, but no mention of the group is found after that.

The Kansas Sheep Breeders and Wool Growers Association was formed in 1881, and breeders of trotting horses organized four years later. Livestock raisers of all kinds were called to a meeting in Topeka in January of 1890, where they combined into what was known as the Kansas Improved Stock Breeders Association.

Stockmen of Barber and Comanche Counties organized the Salt Fork Livestock Association in 1896, apparently for the sole purpose of fighting cattle thieves. The group published a brand book that contained 107 brands. The very next year a new book was published that contained 143 brands. Cattle brands had been published in local newspapers as early as 1882.

The Kansas Livestock Association (KLA) was formed in 1894, when over one hundred Flint Hills ranchers met in Emporia to discuss business problems. On nearly every rancher's mind was the problem of cattle lost to rustlers. Another topic was the high freight costs that the railroads were charging.

Through the years, the KLA addressed many issues that were important to their membership. Some of these were: a state indemnity for ranchers who lost animals due to hoof and mouth disease in 1915, alleged market manipulation by packers the following year, the Texas fever lawsuit against the federal government in 1926, and the Boston restaurant owners' boycott of beef in 1928.

An activity that was a priority of many of the larger livestock associations was the regular inspection of brands at the major markets in Denver, Omaha, Kansas City, St, Louis, Oklahoma City, San Antonio, and Amarillo. For example, at the Kansas City stockyards, one could have seen inspectors from the Wyoming, Montana, South Dakota, and Texas associations looking over cattle shipped from their states. Stolen or strayed cattle were and are still being found at these markets.

THE MONTANA STOCKGROWERS ASSOCIATION

The first meeting of the Montana Stockgrowers Association (MSA) was held on February 19, 1879, in Helena. Twenty-two members signed the new constitution. R. S. Ford was elected president, and invitations to join were sent to several smaller associations, including those in Madison, Lewis and Clark, Gallatin, Deer Lodge, Choteau, and Meagher Counties.

The Eastern Montana Stockgrowers Association (EMSA) was founded in Miles City in 1883 due to the livestock business expanding into former northern Indian hunting grounds. This expansion resulted in Indian raids on the cattle and ranches in that part of the state.

At the April 3, 1885, meeting of the EMSA in Miles City, representatives of the Montana Stockgrowers Association attended, and the two groups agreed to combine. It was decided that the spring meeting would be held in Miles City and the fall meeting in Helena. The association is still in operation today.

THE NEBRASKA CATTLEMEN ASSOCIATION, INC.

The continued heavy settlement of range lands in turn greatly increased the rate of livestock theft from ranchers. Nebraska cattlemen suffered much the same way as neighboring states with theft and enforcement problems. Cattle thieves who were caught and brought to court faced a jury made up mostly of grangers, who didn't see slaughtering the cow of a rancher as much of a problem. Ranchers, of course, viewed the problem differently. They definitely took exception when rustlers took cattle to start their own herd and when cows were butchered for sale to local meat markets that cared little about the origin of the product.

Frustrated cattlemen began taking the law into their own hands and several suspected rustlers ended up dead in a relatively short time. Knowing this type of activity would only get worse, cattleman and banker R. M. Hampton called a meeting at his bank in Alliance. Albert and Mayre Modisett, A. S. Reed, Bartlett Richards, and John Adams were among the group who attended the meeting in 1888. Hampton asked his fellow ranchers to consider establishing an organization like those in Wyoming and Montana. The men agreed to organize and elected A. S. Reed as president, R. M. Hampton vice-president, and E. H. Searles Jr. as secretary/treasurer. They named the new organization the Western Nebraska Stock Growers Association (WNSGA). They had little trouble in signing up over one hundred members.

Prior to the formation of the WNSGA, Nebraska cattlemen had apparently entered into an agreement with the Wyoming Stock Growers Association (WSGA), who agreed to inspect all Nebraska shipments, hold out stolen or strayed stock, and see that the rightful owner received payment. The cost of this service was $800 annually. Interestingly, the assistant secretary of the WSGA reported some problems with the arrangement in their 1887 published reports:

> *At the annual meeting in 1886 the Nebraska members signified their intention to form an association of their own, and they there-fore, by resolution, exempted from further assessment, as in the case with Montana members the year before. The attempt to organize a Nebraska association proved unsuccessful, and resulted only in unsettling the financial relations previously existing between the Association and its Nebraska members, and materially reducing the income usually derived from the latter source. It is only fair to state that in the majority of cases the Nebraska members have cheerfully responded to the call for assessments, but justice prompts the Committee to report that in one or two instances members of the Association controlling cattle interests in Nebraska continue to avail themselves of the benefits and protection afforded to them by its operations, but refused when called upon to bear their fair share of the expenses incurred.*

In 1889, another group of cattlemen met in Hyannis to form the Northwestern Nebraska Stock Growers Association (NNSGA). Dr. A. J. Plummer was elected president. This group also posted the same reward notice and added a twenty-five-dollar bounty on gray wolves who had been killing cattle.

In 1895 the two organizations merged and operated under the name Western Nebraska Stock Growers Association (WNSGA). On June 1, 1900, the WNSGA was incorporated and the name changed to the Nebraska Stock Growers Association (NSGA). A final name change occurred on August 24, 1988, with the consolidation of the Nebraska Livestock Feeders Association (est. 1970) and the Nebraska Feedlot Council (est. 1987) to the Nebraska Cattlemen Association, Inc.

Other smaller associations existed in Nebraska, as in other states. The Stock Association of the Western District of Nebraska formed in 1875 and required the ownership of at least one hundred cattle and members be a resident of the "western stock district." In 1878 I. P. Olive, who became known as the infamous man-burner, organized the Custer County Livestock Association. In 1879 the Sioux County Stock Growers Association was established but disbanded in 1881. Headquartered in Culbertson, the Southwestern Nebraska Cattle Growers Association was formed in 1879. Records also indicate that the Cheyenne County Stock Association, located at Sidney, existed in the late 1870s and early 1880s.

The Thedford Livestock Association was a noted organization because of its petition to Congress, effecting a change in the 1862 Homestead Act that allowed settlers to claim up to 640 acres of land instead of only 160 acres. O'Neill congressman Moses P. Kinkaid was able to push the amendment through (the Kinkaid Amendment to the 1862 Homestead Act), which went into effect in 1904. This amendment of national law pertained only to Nebraska.

THE NEVADA CATTLEMEN'S ASSOCIATION

The Nevada State Cattle Association was established on December 31, 1935, in Elko. The first president was William B. Wright. Membership fees were one dollar and annual fees were based on the size of operation the member had. The organization was begun to "give group representation and consideration to any and all problems of interest to the cattle and horse growers of the state of Nevada." The current name is the Nevada Cattlemen's Association.

THE NEW MEXICO CATTLE GROWERS ASSOCIATION

On November 17, 1914, stockmen from Grant, Sierra, and Socorro Counties met and formed the Southwestern New Mexico Cattle Growers Association. The organization's purpose was to instill sound principals of breeding and growing cattle, to assist the New Mexico Livestock Sanitary Board in its work to build up the industry, and to promote enforcement of the stock laws of the state. Members agreed to pay reward money for evidence of cattle theft. The advisory board would set the amount to be paid depending on the value of the information.

In 1915 the members approved the payment of rewards for the killing of predatory animals (wolves, mountain lions) on a member's range. The board raised the members' yearly assessment to three and a half cents per head of stock owned, and employed an attorney to help prosecute theft cases of association members' cattle. During the same year, the "Southwestern" was dropped from the name, and a new constitution was drawn up that indicated another name change to the New Mexico Cattle and Horse Growers Association.

By 1917 the association was experiencing growth by more than doubling its membership and by absorbing local organizations. The Albuquerque County Farmers Association, the Watrous and Wagon Mound Cattlemen's Association (a part of the Northern New Mexico Stock Growers Association), and the Central New Mexico Cattlemen's Association joined the state organization.

In 1929 the membership approved a final name change to the New Mexico Cattle Growers Association. One member, unhappy with the change, stated to the assembly, "I hope that when you get home, your horses kick you!"

THE NORTH DAKOTA STOCKMEN'S ASSOCIATION

The North Dakota Stockmen's Association (NDSA) was established in 1929, for the benefit of livestock producers of the state. It was incorporated as a nonprofit corporation in 1941. The NDSA is the state-appointed agency responsible for enforcing livestock laws and brand inspection.

THE OKLAHOMA CATTLEMEN'S ASSOCIATION

In comparison to other western states, Oklahoma's organization is relatively new. The Oklahoma Cattlemen's Association (OCA) was officially chartered on March 6, 1950, by a group of cattlemen in Seminole, and today is headquartered in Oklahoma City. The founding interests of the group are the benefits from having an organized voice representing the cattle producers of the Sooner State. Older groups existed, such as the Osage County Cattlemen's Association (est. 1934), Northwest Oklahoma Cattlemen's Association (est. 1945), the Bluestem Cattlemen's Association (est. 1945), and the Wichita Livestock Anti-Theft Association (est. 1946). By June 1947 an unbelievable thirty-six cattlemen's organizations existed in the state. By 1953 the organizations merged to become active members of the Oklahoma Cattlemen's Association. The concerns that brought them all together were cattle theft, disease, declining prices, drought, and the need for strong legislation.

THE OREGON CATTLEMEN'S ASSOCIATION

The first meeting of the Oregon Cattle and Horse Raisers Association was held in Baker, on May 14, 1913. Baker was chosen because it was the center of commerce for eastern Oregon and much of Idaho, with gold, timber, and cattle ranching as the primary sources of income. They adopted a constitution and laid out their purpose, which was to "improve the circumstances of the people in the industry, to help growers sell enough animals and at a price that would allow them to make a profit." In 1913, a three-year-old steer brought twenty dollars, and cows were selling for fifteen dollars a head. Some of the charter members included William Pollman of Baker, Ed Coles of Haines, Fred Phillips of Baker, Ernest Locey of Ironside, Henry Haas of Enterprise, Garland T. Meador of Prairie City, Charles Wendt of Baker, Otis Elliott of Hereford, George Chandler of Baker, and Jack Tippett of Enterprise.

One of the first problems the association had to address was the revision of old livestock laws. An old system of county brand recording made it possible for thirty-six duplicate brands to exist in the state. They were able to get this system changed with the responsibility of brand registration and recording being assigned to the state veterinarian. Duplicate brands in the state were then prohibited. A brand board was given the task of sorting out conflicts in the three thousand brands used at the time. Gerry Snow, a respected brand inspector working out of Portland, wrote the first state brand book.

Livestock theft was a major problem for the group. At one of the first association meetings, Ed Coles commented about thieves, "They really know their business, my herd of 500 horses loose on the range recently dwindled to 150, the cattle and horse raisers association has got to get tough." The group decided to establish a $1000 reward for the capture of livestock thieves, in addition to their brand inspection program. They also started a fund to pay for special attorneys to prosecute cases of theft involving members' animals. Through the work of the association's attorneys, they were able to obtain rate reductions on livestock freight charges. This reduced schedule was referred to as the Cattle and Horse Raisers Scale. The fight against stock thieves was successful enough to lower the reward to $250.

By 1928 thieves were still a continuing problem, however, becoming very mobile by using cars and trucks to rapidly move stolen livestock out of the area. The association was able to prompt the Oregon legislature into passing an antitheft bill, which helped protect ranchers' investments. The act also gave the state traffic officers the power to enforce more than traffic laws. This eventually enabled them to enforce all laws, which lead to reorganization into the Oregon State Police in 1931.

The Cattle and Horse Raisers Association was renamed the Oregon Cattlemen's Association in 1948. The Oregon State Department of Agriculture assumed the duties of brand recording by the following year. On June 18, 1952, the *Oregon Cattleman* magazine debuted under the auspices of President Harry Stearns of Prineville, and Ed Fallen served as editor.

THE SOUTH DAKOTA STOCK GROWERS ASSOCIATION

South Dakota ranchers had the same problem as other states with live-stock thieves, and because of this, they decided to organize. Three ranchers met in Buffalo Gap in 1892, three years after becoming a state, to establish the Western South Dakota Stock Growers Association (WSDSGA). James M. Wood was elected as the first president, Charles Ham vice-president, and F. M. Stewart secretary. The stated purpose of the organization was to "advance the interests of the stock growers of South Dakota and adjoining states, and for the protection of the same against fraud and swindlers, to prevent the stealing, taking or driving away of cattle, horses, mules, and asses from the rightful owners thereof, and to enforce the stock laws of South Dakota." The name would eventually change to the South Dakota Stock Growers Association in the early 1930s.

During 1894 inspectors claimed 2,014 head of cattle worth $63,044 for its members. Cost of inspections for the year was $1,200. The association paid out $1,195.10 to detectives Joe Elliott, J. M. Coleman, W. E. McCarthy, and Ed Hart.

The association's membership stood at 677 on its tenth anniversary. The inspectors recovered 42,953 estrays worth $1,547,752.67 for the members. Inspection costs were $25,131.53 and $31,835 was paid to detectives.

The first brand book was published by the association in June of 1895, listed all brands owned by members, and described the areas where the livestock would normally be found.

On December 10, 1891, the Missouri River Stockmen's Association was formed at Fort Pierre. Officers were A. D. Merriott, president; G. P. Waldron, vice-president; J. H. Hallet, secretary; and Eugene Steere, treasurer; plus an executive committee consisting of the officers (excluding the treasurer) and Scotty Philip, M. E. Williams, John Robb, and H. A. Scovel. The association posted a $200 reward for information on rustlers and organized a spring roundup for 1892. They hired inspectors who were assigned to Pierce, Chamberlain, and the Lower Brule and Crow Creek Reservations.

The Fall River County Stock Growers Protective Association was also formed in 1891, with Joe Marty as president and William F. Wyatt as secretary. (Marty later became the first elected sheriff of Fall River County.) Dues were fifty cents, but membership was open only to those owning or controlling fewer than a thousand head of cattle or horses. By the following year the group had eleven branch lodges, totaling 141 members. On March 5, 1892, the group incorporated and dropped "protective" from the name. Their first brand book, published by the Hatchet Publishing Company of Hot Springs, was thirty-two pages long and included 210 different brands. The book's cover was red and stamped with the owner's brand.

At least three organizations used the Black Hills Stock Association name during the 1880s and 1890s, one of which was started at Rapid City in 1892 by James P. Black. Newspapers of the time often reported the names of these associations incorrectly, making it appear that more groups existed than actually did. By 1905 there was a Southwestern South Dakota Livestock Association, which was rumored to having been established to break up the main association (the WSDSGA), but this did not happen.

In 1928, some stockmen felt that the WSDSGA couldn't financially handle employing range detectives any longer, so they established the West River Stock Growers Protective Association at Philip. The stated purpose was "for more effective and expeditious law enforcement." G. E. Wilkinson was president, Ernest Eidson vice-president, and Anderson Michael secretary/treasurer. The group succeeded in getting Jim Twiford and Tom Petty appointed as deputies under State Sheriff Fred Minier, for the purpose of livestock theft enforcement. This group was eventually absorbed by the WSDSGA, which later became the South Dakota Stock Growers Association.

TEXAS AND SOUTHWESTERN CATTLE RAISERS ASSOCIATION

The Texas and Southwestern Cattle Raisers Association (TSCRA) got its start at Graham, Texas, in 1877, when forty cattlemen held a meeting. The original name, the Stock Raisers Association of Northwestern Texas, was organized to fight cattle rustlers who were destroying their herds.

Charles Goodnight, cattleman and plainsman, helped to organize the Panhandle and Southwestern Livestock Association in Mobeetie during 1881. Goodnight was known for his strict adherence to warnings given by Panhandle stockmen to rustlers, as well as those moving herds of fever-ridden cattle. He once wrote to a friend who planned to drive a herd north through the Goodnight range. He wouldn't take the chance of exposing his already sick herd to his friend's fevered cattle. He told his friend that his herd would be shown a route diverting them from his range, and if he chose not to take it, to inform his men what would happen to them. He reportedly told him that their friendship wouldn't protect him if he drove through Goodnight range. This became known as a "Winchester quarantine."

In 1893, the northwestern organization changed its name to the Cattle Raisers Association of Texas, and in so doing, took in many new members from small county organizations. In 1921, at the request of the Panhandle and Southwestern, the name was changed to the Texas and Southwestern Cattle Raisers Association. The TSCRA is now a large association with membership throughout the southwestern United States. Their stock inspectors were commissioned as "Special Texas Rangers," beginning in 1893.

THE UTAH CATTLEMEN'S ASSOCIATION

In 1885, the year that the Utah Cattle and Horse Growers Association (UCHGA) was formed, the January 11 issue of the *Salt Lake Herald* made a statement that summed up the need for such an organization: "Mutual protection against thieves will be a great advantage to all over the old way of every owner watching his own interests, caring nothing for those of others."

At the time, seven counties had formed local associations. Joel Grover, secretary of the newly formed UCHGA, aptly stated, "Counties could not individually afford to station agents and inspectors at camps where thieving was liable to be carried on, but if they united into a territorial organization, they could clearly afford it."

In April of 1885, the local and territorial associations met in two separate locations in Salt Lake City. Officers of the groups met to discuss combining. The topic of including sheepmen to the membership brought hot argument, some stating that it wasn't possible for cattle to live where sheep had fed. The result of this battle was the formation of the Territorial Stock Growers Association of Utah, which meant two territorial groups existed at the same time. Many frustrated members admitted having two associations was better than the previously unorganized territory. It was said that losses to thieves were so high that it could justify the employ of dozens of detectives.

The current group, the Utah Cattlemen's Association (UCA), was organized in 1890. The UCA provides a collective voice for the interests of ranchers across the state. The association's activities include advertising campaigns encouraging people to eat beef, and legislative lobbying for laws that favor public grazing and ranchers' rights.

THE WASHINGTON CATTLEMEN'S ASSOCIATION

The Washington Cattlemen's Association (WCA) was organized in 1925. The group is dedicated to providing a unified voice for beef producers, promoting rangeland livestock management, and protecting and preserving the cattle industry. The *Ketch Pen* is the official publication of the WCA and is published ten times per year. It reaches two thousand people involved in the Washington beef industry.

THE WYOMING STOCK GROWERS ASSOCIATION

The first stock association in Wyoming was formed on April 15, 1871, by Ora Haley, Luther Fillmore, Thomas Alsop, Hiram Latham, Charles Hutton, Frank Wolcott, George Fox, and Judge J. W. Kingman. These men met in Laramie and called themselves the Wyoming Stock Graziers Association. Their goals were to negotiate low rates for shipping cattle; to improve the breeds of cattle, horses, and sheep by integrating blooded stock into their herds; to assemble and distribute information and resources for benefit of the members; and to organize for the purposes of protection from the wholesale theft and killing of members' livestock. John A. Campbell, the first governor of Wyoming Territory, served as their president. The stock graziers instituted some organizational procedures that the later Wyoming Stock Growers Association (WSGA) would continue. These consisted of the appointment of a vice-president for each of three counties, Laramie, Albany, and Uinta. Chosen to hold the position of secretary was Major Frank Wolcott, a man who became well known in Wyoming history.

The association also knew that they would have to cultivate politicians who would fight for much-needed legislation to benefit the cattlemen. After meeting in a joint session of the territorial legislature, the first laws dealing with livestock were enacted, most particularly those for the protection of livestock and outlining penalties for offenses against livestock. Although making great strides for the cattle industry, the association would soon realize that making new laws wasn't the hard part. The difficult task of enforcement would take them through many trials and tribulations.

The loss of stock to thieves brought a handful of men to meet in a livery stable in Cheyenne, purportedly to form a "vigilance committee." Among the men who formed the Livestock Association of Laramie County in 1872 were Robert S. Van Tassell, Charles Coffee, and John and Thomas Durbin. This little group had the most influence in what would later be the WSGA.

Yet another group would form an organization that would eventually be absorbed by the WSGA. On November 29, 1873, Laramie County cattlemen John and Thomas Durbin, Charles Coffee, George and Gilbert Searight, H. B. Kelly, Alexander and Thomas Swan, A. H. Reel, John Hunton, T. A. Kent, John Coad, Mark Boughton, and W. L. Kuykendall (who acted as secretary) met in Cheyenne for the purpose of forming the Laramie County Stock Association. On March 28, 1879, a special meeting of the association was scheduled and advertised in the Cheyenne newspaper as "taking the place of the annual meeting scheduled for April 1st." At this meeting, an election of officers was held, the first and last history of the association, and an amendment to the constitution was made. It changed the name from the Laramie County Stock Association to the Wyoming Stock Growers Association. Many new members were admitted at the meeting, but only after careful screening. This practice has continued to the present day. The WSGA was undoubtedly the most powerful and controversial stock association in the West. The first detective-inspector hired was T. M. Overfelt in 1874. During the next two years, Henry DeVoe and J. H. Liggett also signed on.

Thomas Sturgis, WSGA secretary, reported to the WSGA Executive Committee that in 1881 the inspector-detectives had inspected 250,000 cattle and recovered over two thousand head of livestock (cattle, horses, and mules) belonging to members, worth $80,000. The inspector force had grown from one person in 1877 to thirteen in 1881.

A special meeting of the association was held on November 9, 1883, to address certain issues concerning cattle theft. The membership approved the formation of an official "Detective Bureau" and gave the WSGA Executive Committee authority to raise members' assessments as they saw fit and to cover the expenses of their stock detectives. During this meeting, a resolution was passed that established a "black list." The list would contain names of men who had been with the association and were stealing cattle, information that was to come from observations or reports of stockmen. The list would be supplied to all members on a periodic basis. The resolution did include an appeal process for those who desired to have their name removed from the list.

The WSGA was successful in getting the "Maverick Bill" passed, which stated that a maverick included any cattle, or calf running without a mother, without a brand, regardless of having any earmark or waddle. The new law authorized the association to establish dates for spring and fall roundups (any other roundups would be illegal), and all mavericks caught would be sold at public auction, with the proceeds going to the WSGA to help finance the Detective Bureau. The big cattlemen were pleased with the law, but the small ranchers were outraged as they needed mavericks to help increase their herds and resulting income. This action further entrenched the enemies of what was considered the "controlling association."

The WSGA used different techniques to police problems on the range. Upon the request of a member who lived near Rawlins, Detective Chief N. K. Boswell was instructed by the WSGA Executive Committee to enlist a person who wouldn't be connected with the association for the purposes of looking into cattle stealing in that area. The secretary explained in a letter to the member, "Unfortunately all our best detectives are too well known to be of much service to us in a case of this kind so near home." He went on to tell the member they would be sending an outsider to settle in the area to work on the case, and agreed that the association would pay the difference in wages paid by the member and $100 per month, for the man while employed. A Frank Coulter, of Nebraska, was sent a letter by the secretary, requesting, "You and your wife start west with your wagons and horses and come in the direction of Cheyenne, where instructions will be given you as to your destination."

Other associations in Wyoming included the Albany County Stock Association, which existed in 1911, and the Northern Wyoming Farmers and Stock Growers Association, organized in 1892 by a Johnson County group. They were suspected by the WSGA to be cattle rustlers.

CHAPTER 5

The Stock Detectives

STOCK DETECTIVE. IT WASN'T A VERY WELL-KNOWN JOB, UNLESS YOU were a cattleman. Men (and at least one woman) who rode the cattle ranges in search of the unsavory souls stealing and butchering livestock were known by various titles. They were known simply, as those mentioned previously, as (live)stock detective or range(land) detective. Sometimes they were referred to as brand inspector, stray picker, or protection man. In *Triggernometry*, by Eugene Cunningham, the definition was stated rather bluntly: "Some of the old timers remark that stock detective was just another name for thief killer."

Some enterprising men went into the stock detective business on their own. An ad in an 1885 Wichita, Kansas, newspaper read, "Frank J. Hess Private Detective and professional stock hunter, strayed and stolen stock a specialty. I am connected with professional men in every town in southwest Kansas. The patronage of the public respectfully submitted. Office Valley Centre, Kansas." Another advertisement appeared in the *Red Lodge Picket* in 1901: "Montana Live Stock Detective Agency. All stock either strayed or stolen recovered. Correspondence solicited. Address J.H. Hall, Secy., Chance, Mont."

Minutes of a meeting of the Wyoming Stock Growers Association (WSGA) in the late 1870s, defined the title like this: "inspectors and detectives were synonymous in their functioning as well as in name." It was explained that in the early days of the association there was no clear separation of the duties performed by an inspector and those of a detective. An inspector might only go about inspection duties, and a detective might complete only the investigation of crimes. Most of the time, however, one man did both jobs.

An early inspector for the Texas and Southwestern Cattle Raisers Association (TSCRA) described what made a good stock inspector: "they must be of good moral character, industrious, and capable of filling the position, must be a practical cowman, good and quick on marks and brands, and must be strictly temperate and sober."

In the early 1880s, Wyoming territorial law did not clearly delineate the actual authority of the association's enforcement activities. In some cases, inspectors were also sworn deputy sheriffs in the county they primarily worked in. The WSGA decided to give their inspector-detectives a power of attorney, which would enable them to replevin livestock. Additionally, they were issued an official letter that stated the inspector was duly authorized to recover stolen or lost livestock of association members, inspect hides and ownership papers, and make arrests. The letter was signed by the chairman of the WSGA Executive Committee.

Quite often, these detectives worked in secrecy, often appearing as just another cowboy. Their identity was kept secret from the time they were hired by a ranch, cattle company, or livestock association until their job was finished. The secretary of the WSGA stated to the members at their annual meeting in 1884, in regard to their detectives, "Much of their work is of such a nature as cannot be properly discussed in detail. It is sufficient to say that their efforts have been widely directed and have been remarkably successful." He finished with, "The committee are satisfied with the work of the [detective] bureau and believe that it need only be continued with equal energy for a reasonable time to free the country of the men who make a profession of cattle stealing." This assertion was, of course, just hopeful thinking.

Working in secrecy was often advantageous to the detective's success, as he could infiltrate a group without his intent being known. Keeping the employer's identity a secret was necessary when the work resulted in the death of a rustler who couldn't be stopped any other way. These killings were meant to send a message to others in the same line of work.

The attributes of a good stock detective made it necessary to be a knowledgeable cowboy with courage and drive. Many had past experience as a peace officer, which was advantageous. Once accepted, whether as a ranch hand or a member of a separate group, he would watch for rustling activity and keep records until the time came when he would take the thief into custody and deliver him to the local sheriff.

When working for ranches, cattle companies, and associations, the detective was a private officer, unless state law indicated otherwise, having no actual arrest powers other than those bestowed upon every citizen of the republic, which allows a private citizen to arrest another person for an offense committed in his presence. The stock detective would have to testify in court as to what he witnessed, and with a good prosecutor and jury, he hoped to convict the thief.

Unfortunately, even with solid evidence, convicting and sending a cattle rustler to prison was somewhat rare. In the book *Lone Star Man, Ira Aten: Last of the Old Texas Rangers*, a story was related about the rangers arresting six rustlers whom they caught red-handed with a herd of stolen cattle. The jury failed to convict them and let them go. It was the opinion of the day that it was about impossible to convict rustlers. Sometimes juries were afraid of retaliation by the thieves or the thieves' friends if they voted to convict. Also, many juries were made up of grangers, often no friends of ranchers, who even looked at the large ranchers as enemies because of disputes over land and water rights.

As late as 1898 the problem continued. Even though an Arizona newspaper lauded the arrest and conviction of livestock thieves James Kerrick and William Cameron in December of that year, they didn't fail to point out the usual record of the courts. Explaining that if all courts handled cases this way, they believed that cattle thieves would lose interest in their endeavor and pointed out that "It is because they are too leniently handled that causes organized gangs to be formed for the purpose of raiding ranges and isolated ranches ... too often the right parties are arrested and brought to trial, only to be turned loose on some slight technicality."

But, on occasion, a jurist would stand rightfully in the performance of his duties. In 1907 rustling was still a major problem in northern Nebraska. It was considered that the district was infested by livestock thieves and other criminals worse than any other part of the state. When the district judge, W. H. Westover, took the bench in Holt County, there had been no previous convictions of rustlers. So frustrated were the livestock owners that they had to expend the time and money to chase down rustlers themselves. When Westover first took the bench, there were nine vigilance committees who resorted to lynchings as a way to discourage the thieves. A prominent local stockman told the newspaper that he personally knew of twenty-three cattle thieves who were sent to prison during Westover's first year on the bench.

The detective-inspectors also patrolled the ranges of their employer. They made their presence known at sales and stockyards where cattle were assembled for rail shipment. If any livestock was located that he held a vested interest in, he would order them cut out of the herd and held. The detective would then attempt to discover the name of the person or persons trying to dispose of the stock. If the stolen cattle were found at a legitimate sale ring some distance from home, he might decide to allow them to be sold and retrieve the proceeds or have them sent to his employer. It was common for strays to join a herd during cattle drives to these locations and the detective undertook the same retrieval procedure in those cases.

Stock detectives had to be especially proficient in "calling the brands," that is, being able to decipher, or read, a brand to determine the owner. Most detectives carried their own notebooks or brand books, but the best had dozens of brands memorized so, at a glance, they could identify the owner. When a steer had many different licit brands due to ownership changes, his job was to trace through them and find the "holding" brand. The holding brand was the most recent one and indicated the current owner.

Larger cattle associations were able to hire market inspectors, which oftentimes were the stock detectives themselves. The market inspectors were stationed at major livestock markets in Omaha, Kansas City, Chicago, Denver, St. Joseph, Wichita, Oklahoma City, and Fort Worth, where it was their job to watch for their employer's cattle. For economy's sake, some associations would pay another state association to act as their inspector in faraway markets. They also entered into mutual agreements, where they would inspect each other's livestock.

The problem of stock theft was so prevalent that enforcement at the state government level arose. In 1885 the Montana Board of Stock Commissioners was created by the territorial legislature. The governor appointed six commissioners to the board: Granville Stuart, president; Russell B. Harrison, secretary; J. S. Day, R. P. Walker, F. Robertson, and A. A. Ellis. Stuart and Harrison were also officials of the Montana Stockgrowers Association. The board had been authorized to "appoint such stock inspectors and detectives as they may deem necessary for the better protection of the livestock interests of the territory." Seven stock inspectors were hired at a flat $125 per month. No extra money was allowed for expenses and the inspectors had to supply their own horse and related equipment. The 1885 laws of Montana Territory required "Said stock inspectors and detectives, so employed shall each make and execute a bond, with two sufficient sureties, in the sum of three thousand dollars to the territory of Montana, conditioned for the full and faithful discharge of their duties."

The law delineated the duties of inspectors in section 9:

Said stock inspectors and detectives are hereby empowered, and it shall be their duty, to arrest all persons who shall violate the stock laws of the territory which shall come under their observation, and shall upon information that any person or persons have committed any crime or misdemeanor against the laws of this territory, in feloniously branding or stealing any stock, or any other crime or misdemeanor under any of the laws of this territory, for the protection of rights and interests of stock owners, make the necessary affidavit for the arrest and examination of such person or persons, and shall, upon warrant issued therefore by any officer authorized to issue same, immediately arrest such person or persons, and bring them before the officer issuing said warrant, or to any other officer authorized to act in case of absence or inability to act, to be dealt with according to law, and shall make due return of said warrant, and notify said board of stock commissioners of his acts and doings in that behalf.

Districts were set out in section 16:

For the purposes of this act, this territory shall be divided into two districts, and the counties of Dawson, Custer, and Yellowstone shall compose the first district, including also any counties that may be formed out of portions of said counties; and the counties of Meagher, Choteau, and Lewis & Clark shall compose the second district . . . and the stock inspectors and detectives are hereby made district officers, and said board of stock commissioners shall, in all cases, designate the district in which said inspectors and detectives shall serve, which shall be designated in their commissions.

The 1885 territorial laws specified that

It shall be unlawful for any person to brand or mark any calf or other cattle that are running at large, between the first day of August and the first day of September of each year, and between the fifteenth day of November of each year and the fifteenth day of the month of May following: Provided, that any owner of stock may brand, on his own premises, at any time, in the presence of two responsible citizens. Any person violating the provisions of this act shall be deemed guilty of a misdemeanor, and, on conviction of any court of competent jurisdiction, shall be punished by a fine not less than twenty-five dollars nor more than one hundred dollars, for each and every animal thus branded, or by imprisonment in the county jail for a term not exceeding six months, or may be punished by both such fine and imprisonment, in the direction of the court.

The new laws allowed that Missoula, Deer Lodge, Silver Bow, Beaverhead, Madison, and Jefferson Counties, and also all that part of Gallatin County lying west of the summit of Belt or Bridger ranges of mountains, be exempt from this provision. The state prison was located at Deer Lodge and some newspaper comments about brand burners read, "We hope that these miscreants who are increasing their bands by substituting their own brand for those of rightful owners, will be speedily *Deer Lodged.*"

The first Montana detective-inspectors were Thomas A. Mathews, W. D. Smith, J. L. Cox, C. W. Barney, William "Floppin' Bill" Cantrell,

Chandler Smith, and W. P. Clark. A tip of the hat to Montana's detectives appeared in the form of an amusing note in the January 10, 1885, edition of the *Daily Yellowstone Journal*: "The all-seeing eye watches over the people on the sea, but it is the stock detective that gets away with the Montana cattle stealer."

The board of stock commissioners' first report to the governor was for the years 1885–1886, and included these favorable comments:

> *Inspectors of stock have been appointed in all of the counties embraced in the Act, and such inspectors have uniformly performed their duties in a painstaking manner, and the general results have been beneficial, not only to the stockmen in such counties, but throughout the Territory. The stock detectives have rendered material aid in the enforcement of the law and the capture and conviction of offenders, not only against the stock interests of Montana, but in the general enforcement of its criminal laws; and in this connection it should be stated that the moral effect of having inspectors acting in various localities has been of very great benefit in the way of the prevention of crime of all kinds. The benefits derived in this way from the system are almost as important as the direct and more apparent ones.*

During 1886, 119,620 head of cattle were inspected by nine inspectors; 1,659 strays recovered, and 43 persons were arrested. The service given cattlemen by the detective-inspectors was a good value, as the report's statement of expenditures indicated:

Stock Inspectors—First District

C.W. Barney, July 10, 1885 to April 1, 1886	*$1,084.82*
J.L. Cox, July 19, 1885 to April 1, 1886	*1,044.64*
J.H. Lander, September 4, 1885 to April 1, 1886	*932.14*
T.A. Matheus(sic), April 17, 1885 to April 1, 1886	*1,101.14*
W.D. Smith, July 22, 1885 to April 1, 1886	*1,031.25*
C.L. Talbot, Aug., Sept., Oct., and Nov.,	
four months at $70	*280.00*
Total	*$5,473.99*

Stock Inspectors—Second District

Wm. Cantrell, August 4, 1885 to April 1, 1886	*$986.60*
Wm. P. Clark, July 8, 1885 to April 1, 1886	*250.00*
Chas. D. Hard(sic), September 10, 1885 to	
February 10, 1886	*625.00*
Chandler Smith, Aug. 20, 1885 to Dec. 20, 1885	*500.00*
Total	*$2,361.60*

The report indicated that for the year ending December 31, 1886, the Board of Stock Commissioners received $15,429.37, which was contributed by Choteau, Custer, Dawson, Lewis and Clark, Meagher, and Yellowstone Counties.

Some of the most famous Montana stock inspector/detectives, 1886. Pictured are, back row, left to right: J.L. Cox of the Crow Reservation, Charles D. Hand of Lewis & Clark County, William "Floppin' Bill" Cantrell of Meagher County. Front row, left to right: Harry Lander of Teton County, C.W. Barney of Yellowstone County, Wilson D. "Billy" Smith of Custer County and Thomas A. Mathews of Dawson County. COURTESY MONTANA HISTORICAL SOCIETY, HELENA

One interesting entry in the general expense section indicated that on December 10, 1885, stock inspector badges were purchased from S. D. Childs & Co. of Chicago for $22.75 (probably the badges visible on the Montana inspectors shown in the group photograph).

Thieves occasionally tried to employ a scheme like Jim Rey did. In 1890, E. E. Fowler of Bozeman reported that his horse had been stolen from the post where he had tied it. He offered a reward of $10 for the horse, saddle, and bridle. That evening, Rey brought in the horse, claiming to be a stock detective. When asked about the saddle and bridle, Rey said that he knew where they were but it would take more than $10 to get them. The *Anaconda Standard* explained that "Rey was put in charge of the marshal and will be charged with horse stealing unless he brings in the other things."

Enterprising rustlers in eastern Oregon expanded their career possibilities in 1906. Elmer and Al Turner were arrested in nearby Weiser, Idaho, for counterfeiting. They were members of a notorious rustling gang credited with being one of the most successful and skillful that ever operated in eastern Oregon and consisted mostly of sons of highly respected pioneers. The gang had been arrested in 1894 by Umatilla Indian police while driving fifty head of stolen cattle from Union to Weston County.

Rustlers didn't always fit the archetypical portrayal of the stealthy, fast-riding thief of the Old West. In 1905 ranchers complained to the North Dakota cattlemen's association that stock was being run off their ranges. Two stock detectives were soon at work and ran down one rustler with a small horse herd. The thief was so forthcoming about his part of the operation that the detectives allowed him to help round up the stolen horses so they could be returned. Taking advantage of the situation, the thief whipped his horse into a run for freedom. As the *Bismarck Daily Tribune* reported, "He was promptly shot down by the stock detectives." The detectives found some letters on the dead man that, with very little study, enlightened them about the rustling operations. The system they used was that one man would run off some stock, drive them a short way to the second man, who would keep them moving to a third man, and so on, so no one person would be in possession for long, allowing the thieves to remain close to home. One letter was from a Williston banker, who urged the rustler to hurry as he had a buyer waiting. He was the first to be arrested. Certain county officials in both states were also suspects and the investigation continued.

Stock detectives were sorely missed when there were vacancies in the position. Butte, Montana, experienced a rash of horse thefts in 1901, and without a detective, it left the job to ranchers. A gang was operating in the area that stole horses for the sole purpose of supplying eastern packing houses who engaged in canning horse meat. Rancher A. J. Robinson was notified that a man had roped one of the horses on his own range. Robinson waited in hiding at a local barn, as he felt the thief would bring the horse in to sell. About midnight, just as he had expected, the man arrived with the stolen horse. Apparently this was the second time in three weeks that the same scenario had unfolded, with Robinson capturing the thief. The Butte newspaper tersely commented that "In view of the fact that there is no stock detective . . . it may become necessary for ranchers and other horse owners to protect themselves against the ravages of the gentry by organizing and rubbing a few of them off the map."

And speaking of horse theft, in 1906 authorities in Montana received word that stockmen and detectives in Alberta, Canada, were tracking one of the most dangerous gangs of horse thieves that ever operated in the West. The fifteen-member gang would steal horses and take them into Canada, and some were sold back into Montana. A Canadian stock detective tracked down R. J. Lockwood, alias Charles Owens, to a point north of Regina where the thief was found with eight of the one hundred head that had been stolen. Lockwood was taken to a Royal Northwest Mounted Police barracks and held. It was said that more stock had been stolen during the past two years in western Canada than at any time in the history of the stock industry there.

Probably the most bizarre situation an inspector ever encountered was reported by a Holdrege, Nebraska, newspaper in June 1884. It all began as rancher John W. Ellis and his cowboys rounded up cattle. Ellis's ranch was near Max, Nebraska, in Dundy County. As they worked, "They were startled by a terrific whirring noise over their heads, and turning their eyes saw a blazing body falling like a shot to Earth. It struck beyond them, being hidden from view by a bank." Herdsman Alf Williamson was burned when he got too close to the smoking object, and had to be taken to the ranch house for care. Southwest Nebraska Cattle Growers Association brand inspector E. W. Rawlins was the only official available to ride out and see it. He noted in his journal, "the aerolite or whatever it is, seems to be about fifty to sixty feet long, cylindrical, and about ten or twelve feet in diameter. Great excitement exists in the vicinity and the round-up is suspended while the cowboys wait for the wonderful find to cool off to examine it. Mr. Ellis is here and will take the first train to the land office with the intention of securing the land on which this strange thing lies, so that his claim cannot be disputed." Unfortunately, a hellacious rain storm came the next day, and either washed the numerous metal pieces away down the gully or "dissolved" them, as it was reported in a few newspapers. Some blamed the event on the imaginative minds of newspaper reporters, to prop up sales or just to entertain readers but, whatever happened there in Dundy County in 1884, it is credited for being among the first UFO sightings in the West!

Rustlers pillaged Indian reservations as well, to such a degree that the US government appointed federal stock detectives to reservations. Thieves included both whites and Indians. One amusing case occurred on a Sioux reservation in South Dakota. In November 1908, Joshua Roan Eagle "eloped" with a neighbor's "squaw" and six horses. They sold two horses at Philip, then went on to Cottonwood where the rest were sold. Six months later Roan Eagle reappeared in tow of government stock detective R. H. Sands and Deputy US Marshal J. E. Parmley. Roan Eagle faced commissioner W. S. McLain in Philip and it was reported that "he will doubtless spend from three to five years in the Sioux Falls penitentiary for his folly." There was no report on what happened to the eloped wife.

Changes of government stock detectives were often reported in local newspapers. In December 1908, the Rosebud Indian Reservation detective, Captain Jack Foster, died suddenly and John Harty was appointed to succeed him. Newton Splawn got the job on the Rosebud Reservation in August 1912, after serving eighteen months as Tripp County South Dakota deputy sheriff.

Easily the most unprecedented activities that stock detectives were ever involved in would have been the Johnson County War in 1892. This was when the fight against rustlers by the large cattle interests came to a head. Members of the Wyoming Stock Growers Association, some of their stock detectives, and a hired gun army advanced into Johnson County for the express purpose of exterminating on sight any suspected rustlers listed in their "black book." Nate Champion and Nick Ray were killed when the invading army attacked them at the KC Ranch. The invaders were pinned down at the TA Ranch by a huge citizen posse from Buffalo.

A precursor to that extraordinary action occurred in 1889, in what was Carbon County. Only three years previously in Rawlins, Jim Averell met Ellen Watson Pikell and they fell in love. The two traveled to distant Lander to get married as soon as Ellen's divorce was final. It is presumed that they married in Lander where people didn't know them so they could file on two homestead claims instead of one as required for families. Their claims in Sweetwater country, just northeast of Independence Rock, took a chunk of open range land that rancher Al Bothwell had been using. Bothwell challenged the claims to no avail.

In addition to the ranch work, Jim Averell—who had spent most of the 1870s as a soldier in the frontier army—was appointed as local justice of the peace and Sweetwater postmaster. He also operated a small store. Ellen bought thirty head of cattle from a cowman who was driving them down the Oregon Trail.

Early on July 20, 1889, stock detective George Henderson was looking over Ellen's newly branded cattle. He reported back to his boss, cattle baron John Clay, who owned the Quarter Circle 71 Ranch. With this information, Al Bothwell called a meeting of five other ranchers where he promoted the idea that Watson and Averell were rustlers. Not all of the men were convinced, so they all went to Ellen's place and saw the new brands for themselves. With Bothwell's continued persistence, the group forcibly took Ellen and Jim to a secluded spot near Independence Rock and lynched them. A headline in a South Dakota newspaper read, "LYNCHED CATTLE KATE . . . The Notorious Wyoming Cattle Queen Strung Up with Her Paramour."

Twelve years later, the July 3, 1904, edition of the *Saint Paul Globe* ran an article that helped explain the continued fight against rustlers in Johnson County. It was titled "How the Rustlers Were Driven Out at Last." Information had been received from Cheyenne that Tom O'Day, known as the "king of the cattle rustlers," had been captured during the gang's robbery of a Bell Fourche, South Dakota, bank. O'Day had received that title in 1901 after his partner, "Flat Nose" George Currie, was killed by officers in Utah. Currie had moved to Johnson County, Wyoming, from his home at Chadron, Nebraska, to take up rustling full time. They set up a ranch a year or two before the Johnson County invasion in 1892 as a front for their illegal activities. They were known as the "Log Cabin" gang. The article read, "Curry [sic] organized a gang of cattle rustlers and began operating on a wholesale scale. He was an expert in the use of a running iron."

Currie and his lieutenant, O'Day, were associated with the Hole-in-the-Wall gang and expanded their criminal enterprises. The Wyoming Stock Growers Association made it a bit uncomfortable for the Log Cabin gang, so they "gathered" a large herd and drove them north into Montana and established a new base of operations. Pinkerton detectives finally ended Currie's career when they ran down Currie and fellow outlaw Tom Cartwright on the banks of the Green River in Utah.

The article offered a hopeful prediction: "Unless O'Day makes good his threat of breaking out of the penitentiary, the authorities believe that they have finally ended cattle rustling in Wyoming, at least on a wholesale scale." It also explained that the war against rustlers had cost many lives over the previous twenty years, and hundreds of thousands of dollars' worth of livestock had been lost. The article ended, "The cattlemen will welcome the peace that is promised by the capture of the 'king of the cattle rustlers.'"

Women were not commonly victims of lynchings, but it was not unheard of either. Mrs. W. T. Holton was getting ready for bed when men came into her ranch home in a remote part of Keya Paha County, Nebraska, where she "was outraged and lynched." A passerby found the woman hanging the next day. There were two general theories to the murder, the first that she had given evidence against rustlers in the area, and second, and the less believable, was that she was in league with the rustlers and the lynching was carried out by vigilantes. Mrs. Holton was known to be a respectable woman, so the second theory may have been false.

As time progressed, various laws were enacted regarding butchering and animal hides. Occasionally, these laws were violated carelessly, and sometimes intentionally. One of many instances occurred in 1903. Montana stock inspector J. T. Webb arrested Lincoln Hanan for "selling dressed beef in Billings without a butchers' license and without exhibiting the hide of the animal slaughtered to the purchaser of the meat." Hanan was fined $20 and costs.

Presented here, in no particular order, are a few of those stock detectives and inspectors who risked life and limb to police rustlers in the West.

WILLIAM D. "BILLY" SMITH

William D. "Billy" Smith was born in Texas in 1854. He had been a detective for the Wyoming Stock Growers Association when he went to Montana in 1882, at age twenty-eight. Smith accepted a similar position with the Montana association three years later, and served as Custer County deputy sheriff at the same time. He was nominated for an inspector's job by the board of stock commissioners in 1885. He spent 1891 and 1892 inspecting cattle at the Chicago market before returning to Miles City.

In August 1893, Smith tracked three rustlers who'd stolen a herd of horses from the Crow reservation. Standing on a butte in eastern Montana, he kept watch at the hideout they had secreted themselves in, with horses grazing nearby. Considering what strategy he would use to make the arrests, he was pleasantly surprised to see John Armstrong, a stock inspector from North Dakota, and a cowboy with a string of broncs, who were both heading to the Pierre Wibaux ranch on Beaver Creek. Smith engaged their assistance by stationing the two men outside the dugout. Both wondered how Smith planned to get the rustlers to come out. Smith stepped onto the dugout's roof, drew both of his six-shooters, and began firing down into the hideout. The three thieves couldn't stumble outside fast enough. Once outside, they froze in their tracks when they saw the other two men holding cocked pistols on them. When Smith climbed down, he noticed the cowboy was very nervous, so told him to put the pistol away. In his fright, while trying to uncock the revolver, it discharged, killing one of the rustlers' own horses. After handcuffing, Smith took the three to Miles City. They each received a ten-year sentence in the federal penitentiary for stealing about two hundred horses from the Crow reservation.

As a most effective stock detective, notes of his most recent arrest of thieves were not uncommon in the newspapers. One such notice in 1897 told of Smith's arrest of six soldiers, members of the Eighth Cavalry from Fort Keogh, whom he had caught killing and butchering cattle on the reservation. Also that year, two men attempted to spring their friend from jail. Billy Smith was temporarily manning the jail when the men stepped in. He told them they couldn't see their friend until the police sergeant came back in a few minutes. Smith's "boyish face and peaceful expression threw the visitors off their guard," as the Helena newspaper put it. They ignored the soft-spoken Smith and opened the door to the cells. Smith tackled one man as the other headed into the cell block. He managed to shove his opponent into an empty cell, slamming the door just as the other visitor freed their friend. Smith used a hard right to lay out one man and then plowed into the escapee. At the fight's end, all three were securely locked inside the cells. Billy Smith broke a bone in his hand when he laid out one fellow. The paper described the prisoners: "Both the men in the jail are in a bad way, though, and will have headaches for a while that will remind them that one shouldn't always judge by appearances."

In the spring of 1899, Smith, along with stock detectives Harry Lander and John W. Collins, rode to a ranch twenty-five miles west of Glasgow, where they found and arrested P. M. Price. Texas authorities had notified them that they had been looking for the cattle rustler for twelve years. Confronted by the three detectives with drawn guns, Price chose to surrender without a fight.

Once again, the Crow Indians were victims of rustlers. Smith was involved in one assignment in an extremely remote area of the Bighorn Canyon of Wyoming and southern Montana. The area, bounded on the west by the canyon itself, Devil Canyon on the south, and Big Bull Elk

Ridge on the north and east, was part of the Crow reservation. The area was so remote that it took a government agent seven years to track down Samuel Garvin, a resident, to make him pay required fees for the government land lease. The Crow were losing cattle at an unusual rate, and rustlers were suspected. Two other ranchers in the area kept an eye out and found newly branded cattle at Garvin's place. More altered brands showed up and were traced to Garvin, who said the cattle belonged to his foreman. One of the ranchers reported his discovery to law enforcement. Federal agent Edwards, Yellowstone County sheriffs, Crow Indian police, and stock inspector W. D. Smith crossed the frozen Big Horn in the middle of winter 1901 and headed to the basin. There they found 750 Crow cattle with altered brands. Edwards charged Garvin and Robert Lee, his foreman, with the theft. By June a grand jury in Billings indicted Garvin and Lee. Their attempts to pay witnesses to leave the area had been unsuccessful. One day Agent Edwards arrived in Billings by train and was threatened by Lee and one of his cowboys, who held a cocked Winchester rifle on him. Edwards stood firm and the rustlers backed down. Late on Christmas afternoon, the jury brought back a guilty verdict for stealing Indian cattle. Both Garvin and Lee were given one year in the state prison at Red Lodge. Curiously, the remote area where rustler Samuel Garvin lived and plied his trade is named after him. Garvin Basin is now a part of Bighorn Canyon National Recreation Area.

Sadly, other rustlers went to work in the area, many being arrested by Crow Indian police. Agent Edwards estimated the losses to Crow herds from 1884 to 1901 at $250,000, which would be $6.7 million in today's money.

Billy Smith and a posse arrested James Chapple, a member of a wanted rustler band. As their search continued, a confederate shot at the men, with the intention of freeing Chapple. A 1901 Cody, Wyoming, newspaper reported the result of the encounter: "News has been received here of the killing of Jim McPeck by Stock Detective W.D. Smith of Miles City."

Smith's very active career wasn't over quite yet. One of his cases was noted in the *Miles City Independent* of January 11, 1906. Smith was called to Dickinson, North Dakota, to testify in the case of one H. B. Schaff-ner, who had been convicted of cattle theft and fined $500. Schaffner had slaughtered a cow with the brand of G. Bonnanas, claiming it was his own but had been illegally rebranded by Bonnanas. Stock detectives Smith and Twible investigated and found that Schaffner had told the truth, which resulted in the arrest of Bonnanas.

Smith had to resign as stock detective and deputy sheriff because of failing health in 1907. The explanation of his ill health was the result of being shot so many times. William D. "Billy" Smith died in 1915 at age sixty-one in Miles City.

JAMES L. COX

James L. Cox, appointed by the Montana Board of Stock Commis-sioners in 1885, served as inspector on the Crow Indian reservation. Although Cox only worked as an inspector for seven months before resigning, he made ten arrests during that period. Only two weeks after accepting the position with the board, Cox made two arrests in a case already over a month old. The case resulted in the recovery of four stolen horses and the solving of an arson to a barn where several cattle perished along with other property. The *Yellowstone Journal* of April 17, 1886, reported the case:

> **CAPTURE OF HORSE THIEVES**
> *About the 18th of last February Mr. J.W. Chapman of this city had three horses stolen and Mr. S.H. Orr had one taken from their ranch. Through the efforts of Territorial Stock Inspector J.L. Cox, of Miles City, the horses have been recovered, the thieves captured and brought to this city. Their names are Henry Myers and J.B. Moore, both young men, apparently not over 21 years of age, but old in crime, both having a weakness for horse flesh and both have served a term in the territorial penitentiary for horse stealing. . . . The capture of these horse thieves has led to the discovery of the parties implicated in the burning of Saville's barn by which he lost a large number of cows and considerable other property. Myers has confessed that "Tex" Edwards hired him to set the fire to Saville's barn and that he did it.*

Tex Edwards, who was under indictment for not recording brands of slaughtered cattle, was immediately arrested for arson. Myers was also charged with burning the barn. The newspaper went on to commend Inspector Cox for his work:

Stock inspector Cox is entitled to a great deal of credit for the diligence he has exercised in capturing these thieves and in bringing to light the parties who set the torch to Saville's property.

WILLIAM "FLOPPIN' BILL" CANTRELL

It has been said that William "Floppin' Bill" Cantrell was so named for the way he chopped wood for riverboats on the Missouri River, or maybe because of the way his arms flopped when he rode. Bill was from Missouri and rode with Quantrill's guerillas during the Civil War. After the wood-chopping work, he joined up with Granville Stuart's DHS Ranch. He was commissioned by Granville Stuart as a stock inspector for the board in Meagher County, Montana. Cantrell made four arrests in 1885, one in 1886, and was known to have problems getting along with other inspectors. He was a member of "Stuart's Stranglers," as they became known, during the famed vigilante raids of rustler hideouts on the Musselshell and Missouri Rivers in 1884. This dangerous area of the Missouri River was the northern boundary of Garfield, Petroleum, and Fergus Counties, which had become a natural hiding place for rustlers. Cantrell had lived in the area and was familiar with most of the thieves who ran there. This region, called the "Badlands," was made up of sharply eroding cliffs, cutbanks, and lateral coulees covered with a cottonwood jungle. Missouri River steamboat men didn't care who their customers were as long as they paid cash and served as a source of supplies for the rustler band.

From this headquarters, rustlers stole horses and cattle from stockmen in Montana, Dakota, and Canada. By the 1880s the thieves began taking stock closer to their home base, which raised the ire of the stock growers' association even more. Stockmen had chased the outlaws on several occasions but gave up when they approached the Badlands. A few of the pursuers continued into the outlaws' sanctuary never to be heard from again. The nerve of the rustlers escalated to the point that they attempted to rob a US Army payroll wagon and escort on their way to Fort Keogh on the Yellowstone. The result was one soldier killed and one wounded, but the payroll box made it safely to the fort. This blatant attack on US government property seemed to unite the cattlemen, even those who in the past had been too scared to resist the outlaws.

In July 1884 Sam McKenzie, a half-breed who was known to be a full-time rustler, was found on DHS Ranch property. Cowboys of the DHS caught McKenzie and took him in to the ranch house to see Stuart. No records have been found of the conversation that day, but it must not have gone well for the outlaw as the next day his body was found hanging from a tree next to a road on the Reece Anderson ranch. Before McKenzie's death, however, it was learned that his two accomplices, Rattlesnake Jake and Longhaired Owens, planned to steal the entire horse herd from the IJ Ranch during the night of July 4, when everyone would be in Lewiston celebrating. Jake and Owens arrived in Lewiston on the Fourth, waiting for their associate who would never show. They took part in some of the festivities to kill time while they waited. They later found out from a rider who arrived in town that Sam had been hanged. This threw the two rustlers into a rage. They pulled their guns and started to unmercifully shoot up the town. People scrambled for cover, while others armed themselves and returned a staggering fire that decimated Jake and Owens.

Soon after the spectacle in Lewiston, a meeting was held at the DHS Ranch where it was decided the time had come to organize an attack on one of the rustlers hideouts. Cantrell and a large number of heavily armed and well-mounted men set out for the outlaws' domain. They attacked with such ferocity and swiftness that the outlaws had no time to retaliate. Three men were hung and over sixty stolen horses were recovered. The ranchers made a stop at a cabin near the mouth of the Musselshell River. Jim Downs was only too happy to supply all kinds of information about his rustler cohorts, trying in vain to save his own neck. As no tree was handy, the ranchers secured one end of the rope to Downs's neck, and the other to a large grindstone that stood next to his cabin. Downs and the grindstone, with the rope between them, were thrown into the river. Neither was seen again. Even the *New York Times* took note of Cantrell's activity: "Flopping Bill and his party are making the lives of the horse-stealing fraternity of the upper country a wild and terrible uncertainty."

Plans were quickly worked out for an even larger attack on the outlaws' very headquarters at the Musselshell and Missouri Rivers. It was believed that with the recent hangings and attacks, the thieves would run to their headquarters to dig in. The ranchers found they were right. In the predawn hours, they cautiously slipped into the grass and trees, and onto the immediate rough hills that partly surrounded the little cabin, barn, and corral. It appeared by the horses and tack that most of the group was there, still sleeping in the cabin, as well as in a nearby tent. After dawn, the cabin door finally opened, and out came a man walking slowly toward the trees to answer the call of nature. He approached too closely to one of the hidden raiders, who had no choice but to open the ball. The man sprinted back toward the cabin, but before reaching it, his loosely fastened trousers fell to the ground. He fell face first into a rose bush. He scrambled on his hands and knees into the safety of the cabin. The entire attacking party let loose with deafening blasts. Three men were assigned to take the tent, which to their surprise contained six men instead of the three they believed were there. One of the ranchers fainted dead away as the six rustlers opened fire. The remaining two men stood valiantly and fired their Winchesters as fast as they could, but the men were advancing on them. Extra help arrived in time and the six rustlers took off into the jungle of trees. The shootout at the well-fortified cabin continued throughout the day. The ranchers knew this attack had to be won before dark, as the outlaws could slip out during the night. The decision was made to fire the cabin. One of the attackers made his way to a blind spot behind the cabin and got the fire started. It blazed up the wall and produced a heavy smoke before the men inside could figure out where it was coming from. Minutes later, to avoid the suffocating smoke and fire, the men ran out. Those who weren't shot down surrendered to their doom. By nightfall, the cabin was nearly gone; small flames danced around existing boards, providing just enough light to see the figures hanging from the trees. The worn-out attackers rested on the ground near the smoking cabin.

The Stranglers knew they had to complete this unpleasantness and find the escaped fugitives. After replenishing supplies from a steamboat that was in the vicinity, they set out through the dense vegetation, in which travel proved to be too difficult. They returned to Granville Stuart's DHS Ranch and notified army units stationed downriver to watch for the escaped outlaws. The army was most willing to help, still remembering the attack on their payroll wagon. It wasn't long before the fugitives were captured by the army, with the help of the Indian police. The prisoners could only be turned over to civilian authorities, so a deputy sheriff and posse from Fort Maginnis arrived to pick up the outlaws. Unfortunately, when the posse returned, they had no prisoners with them. They reported that masked men had jumped them during the night and taken them.

Floppin' Bill was discharged by the board in 1890 and returned to Missouri. Bill met an untimely end in 1901 when he was hit by a train in the Kansas City railroad yards.

CHARLES D. HAND

Charles Hand was an inspector for the Montana Board of Stock Commissioners. Hand was born on December 20, 1841, and received his education in Rochester, New York. In 1864, he traveled by ship around Cape Horn to San Francisco. Three years later he moved to Montana and accepted the position of "collector of internal revenues." In 1868, he became a deputy US marshal for four years. He next worked as a special agent for the US Department of the Interior for another four years. By 1875, he had purchased 240 acres of land near Helena and raised thoroughbred horses.

On September 10, 1885, records indicate that Charles Hand was appointed stock inspector for the board. He resigned only a few months later when he was appointed deputy sheriff of Lewis and Clark County. He probably held both inspector and deputy sheriff positions simultaneously for the following few years, which included a two-year stint as city marshal of Helena. About 1889 Hand donated forty acres of land where the new Montana university would be built.

Hand moved on in 1909, settling in Salt Lake City, Utah.

J. H. "HARRY" LANDER

Harry Lander was a man of many places and experiences, including service as an early inspector for the Montana board. He was born on May 1, 1859, in Peoria, Illinois. Through the years his work ran the gamut from cowboy, lawman, cattleman, buffalo hunter, and gold miner to roundup captain and personal friend of Teddy Roosevelt. He was married three times, the first two wives dying in childbirth, and a divorce ending the last one. He was known during his Alaska adventures not only as a gold mine manager but also for having trained his horses to walk with snow shoes. The *Journal* at Miles City noted that "J.H. Lander, one of the prosperous stock growers of Powder River arrived in town yesterday." In 1885 he worked as foreman of the Illinois and Montana Cattle Company but soon found a job with the Montana Stockgrowers Association as a stock inspector and detective. He was adept in tracking down horse thieves. In June of that year, Lander—along with deputy sheriffs James and Frank Conley—were searching the Little Missouri Valley for a gang made up of Woods, Baxter, and Kelley. They returned to Miles City with Joe Campbell, alias Joe Woods, and horses stolen from a sheep ranch on the Tongue River. It turned out that the other two thieves had been jailed in Bismarck.

In March of 1886 Lander was credited with capturing one horse stolen from Cree Indians. The horse had been abandoned by Peigan Indians (one of three original tribes of the Blackfoot Confederacy), who afterwards stole horses from the Fort Belknap Gros Ventres. Two months later, Lander was lauded in the Fort Benton *River Press* for recovering horses stolen from the Milner Livestock Company. He arrested two men—Horace Rastner, alias Jack Williams, and John Wright—and lodged them in the jail at Maple Creek. The paper said, "Mr. Lander has displayed great energy and sagacity in following up this matter at the request of the Milner Livestock Company. His record as a stock inspector proves him to be a tireless and most effective officer, who is in every way entitled to the regard that is entertained for him by the best stockmen."

In July of 1886 he was appointed as an inspector at the Minnesota Transfer Railway Company in St. Paul. A melancholy departure notice was published in the Fort Benton newspaper: "Mr. Lander has done some good work here, having recovered forty-two head of stolen horses and returned them to their owners. In addition to this he has been instrumental in bringing several criminals to justice. While here Mr. Lander has made many friends who will regret his departure."

Even though Lander was in Minnesota, his name made the papers again. A warrant had been sworn out for the arrest of the notorious "Nosey" Smith, who had a fight with Lander over a charge of stealing and killing cattle. Smith's wife told constables, who arrived too late to find him, that Smith had knocked her down, breaking her arm, and attacked his thirteen-year-old daughter, "whom he had also beaten and outraged in the presence of the family." Smith's wife told the officers that he had killed a Frenchman and a sergeant from Fort Shaw. He forced her to help him throw the sergeant's body and gun into the river. She added that he had killed some thirty-six head of cattle, whose hides were seen all over the camp. Apparently, while on the lam, Smith wrote to the paper to dispute the charges made against him by his wife. The *River Press* said in partial response, "Smith does not mention the fact that he tried to kill Lander, the stock detective."

The board decided to station Lander in St. Paul during the whole year, and later Chicago, as the increase in shipments of cattle and horses dictated the need. An illustration of the efficiency of Inspector Lander came about in the arrest of three Montana fugitives. In 1895 Harry had arrested George Trotter for horse theft, but he escaped from jail at Glasgow with Charles Sephic, an accused murderer, and Charles Nelson. The three drifted down the Missouri River on a makeshift raft until they reached Dakota, where they took a stock train to Chicago. They were well on their way to making a clean escape. Unfortunately for them, livestock inspector Lander was on duty at the stockyards where the train stopped. Lander recognized Trotter and arrested all three.

Lander reported back to the *River Press* that in 1897, he and his assistants had inspected 147,972 Montana cattle. By 1900, he had resigned as an inspector for the board.

His name would appear again in 1912, when an article appeared in the *Daily Missoulian*. A lawsuit had been filed against the banks to recover $19,540.36 that Samuel Langhorne Jr., a clerk with the

Montana Livestock Board, had embezzled during 1907–1908. The money came from estray funds belonging to various ranchers. The paper named "J.H. Lander, a stock inspector stationed in Chicago," as another person responsible for another $15,000 in missing funds. The *River Press* reported in part the next day: "For while the committee feels certain Lander embezzled between $12,000 and $15,000, it has only credited him with $11,512. W.G. Preuitt [secretary] paid out $98,755.74 of this money. The sum however, has been accounted for on the books of the state board and of those of the Montana Stockgrowers Association, which from June 1, 1892, until April 1, 1907, handled the estray fund." Lander appears to have been exonerated in the mess by the last line of the article: "This money was paid out by Mr. Preuitt for the salaries of stock inspectors, prosecution of stock thieves and other expenses."

Lander lived into his seventies and died in Michigan.

W. C. "BILLY" LYKENS

The Wyoming Stock Growers Association (WSGA) hired Billy Lykens (sometimes spelled Lykins) in 1877. Lykens was one of the best detectives in the association's history, according to their records. His first monthly report stated, "13 head of horses stolen from Pratt and Jervis ranch. All recovered and delivered to owners." The WSGA was so pleased with the work of Lykens that they let him manage the detective work and hire an assistant who would report to him. It was not uncommon for detectives to change jobs periodically, and even though he worked for the WSGA, he apparently also spent some time in 1879 as a special agent for the Union Pacific Railroad. An assignment during that time involved the attempted capture of a very successful horse thief by the name of Doc Middleton. The many horse thefts credited to Middleton in Wyoming and Nebraska were bad enough, but he liked to steal horses from Indians, which seriously hindered the peace process. The US government took exception to this and hired William H. H. Llewellyn as a special agent with the Justice Department to stop these federal crimes against the Indians. Llewellyn seemed to focus on killing Middleton, however. In July 1879, under the ruse of having Doc sign a pardon, Llewellyn and others arranged a meeting in Doc's neighborhood in northern Nebraska. Billy Lykens hid in some brush next to the trail they would use and planned to shoot the horse thief. As the group approached, Lykens aimed his rifle at Middleton and pulled the trigger, which made a loud snap. The noise of the misfire caught Middleton's attention as Lykens tried again with the same result. By this time, the thief jerked his pistol and fired at Lykens. He dropped the malfunctioning rifle and pulled his own pistol to return fire. Doc was wounded by one of the many wild bullets, but he and his party managed to escape. A few days later, Llewellyn, with other detectives and a detachment of soldiers from Fort Hartsuff, captured Middleton as he convalesced in a nearby hideout.

The Wyoming Stock Growers Association considered Billy Lykens one of their best detectives. COURTESY WYOMING STOCK GROWERS ASSOCIATION-BOX 287-, AMERICAN HERITAGE CENTER, UNIVERSITY OF WYOMING

The next notable chapter in Lykens's career would be his last. Having achieved a reputation of being a bane to rustlers, his involvement in the ambush of Nate Champion and Ross Gilbertson at their cabin near the Powder River in Johnson County, Wyoming, wasn't considered a proud moment. Champion was a well-respected man who had never been accused or arrested for rustling. Apparently his only crime was buying a few cattle to start his own ranch, but he soon showed up on the WSGA black list. The next in a series of unfortunate incidents of what would become known as the Johnson County War, came on an early morning in November 1891. Champion and Gilbertson were asleep in their one-room cabin when the door burst open. Men rushed in, pointing pistols and yelling for them to give up. Nate grabbed for his gun and the men started shooting. He returned fire and drove the men out of the cabin. The darkness of the early morning appeared to have hindered the accuracy of the attackers' aim, as neither Champion nor Gilbertson had been hit. Champion was able to see one of the attackers running away holding his middle. A seriously wounded Billy Lykens was later sent to Missouri, where he died.

A short time later Champion, gun in hand and ready to kill Mike Shonsey, demanded to know who the attackers were. He already suspected that Shonsey, the EK Ranch foreman and stock detective, had been there. It was believed the only reason Shonsey talked was because of how close he'd come to dying at that moment. WSGA stock detectives Frank Canton, Fred Coates, Joe Elliott, and Billy Lykens were named by Shonsey, who immediately notified Canton that Champion had forced him to talk.

Wyoming lawman Nathaniel K. Boswell served as first sheriff of Albany County and Chief Detective for the Wyoming Stock Growers Association. COURTESY AMERICAN HERITAGE CENTER, UNIVERSITY OF WYOMING

NATHANIEL K. BOSWELL

N. K. Boswell was hired by the Wyoming Stock Growers Association in 1883 and placed in charge of their new Detective Bureau. Boswell, or "Boz" as his friends called him, was a well-known and respected lawman in Wyoming. He was born in New Hampshire in 1836, and later lived with an uncle in Wisconsin. Boz went to try his luck at finding gold in Colorado, where he met fellow miner Dave Cook, who later established the famed Rocky Mountain Detective Agency. Boz began his career with the agency.

On May 25, 1869, he was appointed the first sheriff of Albany

County, Wyoming, by territorial governor John Campbell. In the election of 1874, Boz was defeated for the sheriff's post, but the people wanted him for city marshal of Laramie City. He accepted the position and concurrently held a deputy US marshal's commission. In 1876 Boz assisted in the arrest of Jack McCall in a Laramie City saloon. McCall had fled Deadwood, Dakota Territory, after murdering James Butler "Wild Bill" Hickok. The US marshal returned McCall to Dakota, where he was hanged. In October of 1887, after inspecting many roundups and arresting numerous stock thieves, Boswell resigned as chief WSGA detective. He died in 1921 and is buried at Laramie.

BEN N. MORRISON

Ben Morrison, an early WSGA detective, was a participant of the Johnson County War. Morrison worked for the association periodically from 1879 to 1888. His first report to the WSGA (September 1879 through March 1880) portrayed him as a no-nonsense character. Here is an excerpt from that report: "Sept. 22, 1879: Left Cheyenne in search of horses owned by Mr. T.A. Kent. Followed trail to Greybull Creek, in the Big Horn Basin, there lost the trail, picked up three head on my return trip. Arrived at Cheyenne Oct. 19, 1879. . . . Feb. 13th: Left to arrest J.J. McGinnis. Captured him at Fort Laramie. On trip to Cheyenne he attempted to make his escape and met his death. Arrived in Cheyenne Feb. 20th, 1880."

After the shooting, Ben turned the body over to soldiers who were providing an escort and returned to Cheyenne. They apparently didn't want to haul the body back to Fort Laramie, so they had some nearby cowboys bury it. A coroner's jury went to the burial site and disinterred the body. The jury found that McGinnis met his death while trying to escape from an officer who was authorized to arrest him. As a matter of procedure, a charge was entered against Morrison, with the jury finding him justifiable in his actions. This would usually have been the end of the matter except McGinnis's widow showed up in Cheyenne with sworn statements from two Fort Laramie soldiers that were with Morrison. The statements indicated that they thought it looked like murder to them. They were actually just over a hill, out of the direct line of sight of the

Wyoming stock detective Ben Morrison decked out with a Mexican double-loop holster for his Colt and woolies. COURTESY WYOMING STOCK GROWERS ASSOCIATION–BOX 287, AMERICAN HERITAGE CENTER, UNIVERSITY OF WYOMING

inspector and his prisoner, when the shooting took place. Resulting from the pressure brought to bear by the McGinnis family and friends, a grand jury investigation of the killing was initiated. Morrison, while on the trail of horse thieves in Dakota Territory, was notified to return to Cheyenne for court on May 25. A little more than a month later, the grand jurors filed their decision, which included comments about the poor condition of the jail and courthouse, and that some local butchers were careless about following the law, but said nothing about indicting Morrison! His report for that year included this amusing statement: "I have this to say, that the duties of the position which I hold is full of perplexities and inconveniences such as are not and cannot be fully understood except by those who have personal experience in the matter." The *Cheyenne Leader* described Morrison like this:

> *He is a man of medium stature, heavy set, and wears an open, gen-erous countenance. In deportment he is calm, and speaks with an air of honesty that is convincing. He much regrets the killing and is sorry it was necessary.*

TOM HORN

Any history of stock detectives would be remiss in not including Tom Horn, probably the most famous, or infamous, stock detective ever. A man of many colorful experiences during his forty-two years, he had a propensity to exaggerate, a fault that helped lead to his demise.

Born in Scotland County, Missouri, Horn left home at fourteen after a serious argument with his father. He went west to Kansas and then to the Southwest, working for the railroad and driving stagecoaches. He was hired as an army packer at the San Carlos Indian Reservation in Arizona and was so employed during the tracking, and final surrender, of Apache chief Geronimo.

By the late 1880s Horn was working as a Gila County deputy sheriff and reportedly had some involvement in the Graham–Tewksbury feud, which was dubbed "The Pleasant Valley War." Horn headed to Colorado around 1890 and was hired by James McParland, chief of the Pinkerton National Detective Agency's Denver division. He proved to be an efficient operative. Two years later the agency sent him to Wyoming at the request of the WSGA, under the name Thomas H. Hale. US marshal Joseph P. Rankin deputized Hale, who was sent to Johnson County to build cases on rustlers. It was known that the WSGA had hired a Pinkerton man and one from the Turtle Detective Agency to augment the detective-inspector force as secret detectives.

Horn was later hired as a stock detective for John Clay's Swan Ranch. One can't ignore the fact that Clay was the president of the WSGA at the time. The association's position on the issue was: "At no time was Tom Horn employed by the Wyoming Stock Growers Association as a stock detective or in any other capacity, but he was employed by individual Wyoming and Colorado cattlemen."

There can be little doubt as to Horn's willingness and ability to kill for money. His modus operandi was using a rifle for a "target" up to 300 yards away. In 1895 he purchased his favorite rifle, a Winchester model 1894, .30-30 caliber rifle with a half-magazine. He liked the new smokeless powder and reportedly said it was important to a man in his line of work. Regarding his firearms, Horn used pistols too. When finally arrested in 1902, Laramie County deputy sheriff Richard Proctor checked in the guns taken from Horn. These consisted of "two nickeled 5½ barrel .45 caliber 1878 Colt Frontier Model double actions, in slim flap-style holsters."

During 1895 Horn was credited with killing William Lewis and Fred Powell. The men had ranches in the vicinity of John Coble's Iron Mountain Cattle Company. Deputy US marshal and former stock detective Joe LeFors later asked Horn about those killings. He confirmed that he just rode up to Lewis and started firing his revolver, "He was the scardest S.O.B. you ever saw." Powell had been killed with a single rifle shot through the chest.

Horn contracted yellow fever during army service in Cuba and recuperated at John Coble's ranch. By 1900, he was employed by cattle baron Ora Haley. He was sent to Brown's Park in northwest Colorado where Haley was experiencing losses. The result was two dead, Matt Rash and Isom Dart. The rest seemed to have vacated the area.

Horn was said to place a rock under the head of his victims. An interesting side note to this "trademark" was mentioned in *Riding the White Horse Home*, by Teresa Jordan, whose family lived at Iron Mountain for generations. Jordan retells an old story about her great-grandfather, David "Papa Dick" Lannen, who killed two men for stealing cattle from him. The two men were found with stones under their heads. "Horn was glad to take the credit . . . a hired gun will always add another notch or two to his resume," Lannen said.

A compelling meeting with the stock detective was described by cowboy John K. Rollinson in his autobiography, *Pony Trails in Wyoming*. While working for the TY Ranch in the Goshen Hole country, seventeen-year-old Rollinson was on the range practicing his roping skills. After a few tries, his rope found its mark. The rest of the small herd retired over a hill away from the excitement. Rollinson sat his horse, happy with his skills, but wondered how he'd get the rope off the steer. Being in wide open country he was startled when a rider appeared seemingly out of nowhere and stopped beside him. Rollinson felt both fear and humiliation getting caught in a spot like this. The stranger's first words were "What the hell is this?" as he noticed the brand on Rollinson's horse did not match that on the roped steer. His hand rested menacingly on the butt of his holstered pistol. He described the man as being "well built, powerful type, in his late thirties, riding a gray." Before he could speak, the stranger commanded, "Boy, how come you're roping other folk's cattle. Who are you and where you from? Speak up, quick!" The startled cowboy was finally able to explain himself and the stranger seemed to recognize it as the truth. In a more friendly tone, the man asked how he was going to get that rope off of the steer. Rollinson admitted that he didn't know. The man said he would help him this time and removed the rope. The stranger then warned him and said he wouldn't report this to anyone and that he could return a favor some other time. After he shook hands with Rollinson and started to ride away, he said, "My name is Tom Horn and I'm a range detective."

The killing of fourteen-year-old Willie Nickell early on the morning of July 18, 1901, was Horn's undoing. A serious, ongoing dispute between the Nickell patriarch, Kels, and the neighboring Miller family was common knowledge. It was also known that Tom Horn had spent the night at the Millers two days before Willie was killed in the early morning hours as he left his family's homestead. Local schoolmarm Glendolene Kimmell was living with the Millers and was no doubt the reason for Horn's stay in the area.

Deputy US marshal Joe Lefors, who had previously served as a stock detective, was asked by the Laramie County sheriff to assist in the Nickell murder investigation. Lefors, who was aware of the locale Horn had been close to at the time of the killing, sent for Horn on the pretense of a job prospect in Montana. Before Horn arrived at the second-floor US marshal's office in Cheyenne, LeFors posted court reporter Charles Ohnhaus and Deputy Sheriff Leslie Snow behind a side door in the office to record the conversation. Horn's sobriety level at the time of the meeting is debated yet today. Whether he only made boastful, private comments between two tough hombres or it was nothing but the talk of a drunk, incriminating statements about the Nickell killing were taken down by Ohnhaus. The result of the conversation-interview was an arrest warrant issued for Horn. Sheriff Ed Smalley, Deputy Sheriff Dick Proctor, and Police Chief Sandy McNeil arrested Horn without incident.

The trial began on October 10, 1902. Even though the fierce prosecutor, Walter Stoll, was very effective, Horn remained unconcerned and thought the whole affair was ridiculous. Besides, he was sure that his employers would get him out of it. One person even testified that he saw Horn the very morning of the murder, twenty-five miles from where Willie was killed, but freedom was not to be. On October 24, 1902, the jury returned a verdict of guilty of first-degree murder. Just over a year later, the stock detective, who had intimidated so many by his mere presence on the range, was hanged.

Horn's good friend John Coble was one of his last visitors. Coble, so distressed over the situation, could barely talk. Eleven years later, on December 4, 1914, Coble walked into the lobby of the Commercial Hotel in Elko, Nevada. He produced a pistol, which he placed into his mouth and pulled the trigger. Down on his luck, one wonders if Coble had also been carrying a nagging guilt over Tom Horn's execution.

The infamous Wyoming stock detective Tom Horn in the Laramie County jail. He was an imposing figure, tall with dark beady penetrating eyes. COURTESY AMERICAN HERITAGE CENTER, UNIVERSITY OF WYOMING

The subject of Tom Horn's guilt has been debated over the years and is still argued today. Earle R. Forrest wrote in his 1936 book, "The evidence against Horn was very flimsy . . . boasting, especially when intoxicated, was Tom Horn's greatest fault."

The supposition that the Wyoming Stock Growers Association condoned the killing of suspected rustlers is best documented in a letter from stock inspector E. P. Philbrick to the association, which in part says: "They say there are seven of them and all go armed and don't allow anyone to come near their camp . . . they also told the stockmen they were not going to be taken alive. . . . I told them that if the outfit were stealing stock and did not want to be taken alive that I thought it would be a good plan to kill them all and arrest them afterwards." The association's letter of reply to Philbrick said, "If you want to go up and inspect the outfit referred to, you are at liberty to do so and may make your arrangements accordingly. If you need them you can get a couple of men to go with you. If necessary you may carry out your plan of killing them and then arresting them. I do not think they will be a loss to the community." Although morbidly humorous, these letters serve to illustrate the seriousness with which the WSGA—and other associations, for that matter—treated the problem of rustlers.

JOE ELLIOTT

Joe Elliott was born in Dodge County, Wisconsin, on May 2, 1860. By the time Elliott was ten, the family had moved to Minnesota. A couple of years later they picked up and traveled to Yankton, Dakota Territory, where they crossed the Missouri River into Nebraska. The family farmed in Cedar County and were proud of their thirty-bushel-to-the-acre corn crop.

In 1876 Elliott and his brothers started freighting into the Black Hills. They turned back on that first trip because they kept meeting bands of Indians, whom they assumed were coming back from the Custer fight. Elliott split off on his own in the early 1880s and ended up working on a horse ranch in northeastern Wyoming. This led to work on cattle ranches and as a range foreman. When asked by an interviewer about his reputation with a pistol, Elliott told him that as a boy, he had broken one of his fingers, which never worked right after that. Fellow cowboys saw him kill a bad steer with a quick draw and fast shot. Another time, he shot a rabbit that a dog was chasing. He mused, "I could have fired all day and not hit that rabbit again."

During his cattle work, Elliott had several run-ins with rustlers who caused him problems. In 1887, he took a job as stock detective for the Wyoming Stock Growers Association and was posted to Upton. One of the precursors to the Johnson County cattle war was the lynching of horse rancher Tom Waggoner in June 1891. Waggoner was accused of being a notorious horse thief and Elliott claimed that Waggoner stole a team of horses from him. Finding Waggoner in a store one day, Elliott confronted the man and hit him across the face with his hat. In front of witnesses, Elliott swore to "get him." Fellow stock detective Billy Lykens told Elliott about other thefts he believed that Waggoner had committed. (Lykens's lack of actual evidence is probably why he hadn't arrested Waggoner.) After three men took Waggoner away, his body wasn't found for sixteen days. Joe Elliott was part of the search party and found the suspected thief hanging by his neck. Everyone remembered the threat Elliott had made toward Waggoner and were sure he had been in on it. It was believed that an assassination squad made up of Coates, Lykens, and Elliott were the responsible parties. Elliott denied it to his dying day. Strangely, he was appointed to round up the dead man's horses and sell them, with Fred Coates serving as administrator of the estate.

Even though Joe Elliott's life was continually threatened for his role in the Johnson County War, he lived to a ripe old age. COURTESY AMERICAN HERITAGE CENTER, UNIVERSITY OF WYOMING

The next targets were blacklisted cowboys Nate Champion and Ross Gilbertson. In November, the cowboys fought off an attack at their cabin. Sometime later, Champion forced Mike Shonsey at gunpoint to admit who the attackers were. Shonsey named Joe Elliott, Frank Canton, Billy Lykens, and a "Woodbox Jim." More attacks followed before the big cattlemen recruited and organized a group of fifty-two Texas gunmen, WSGA stock detectives (including Joe Elliott), and ranchers to invade Johnson County, believed to be the main nest of rustlers, and kill them as they found them. Their attack on the cabin of Nate Champion and new partner Nick Ray was successful this time. But Johnson County residents had formed a huge posse that cornered the "invaders" at the TA Ranch, forty-five miles south of Buffalo, the county seat. A US Army detachment was sent for from Fort McKinney while the battle raged. Upon arrival at the TA, the soldiers took the invaders into custody and escorted them to the fort. They were transferred to the territorial prison at Laramie for a short time and then to Fort D. A. Russell near Cheyenne. The trials went on for months, but after the defense eliminated nearly every suitable man in Cheyenne to serve on the jury, the legal action went nowhere. By ones, twos, and fours, the cases were dismissed. Not one member of the invader group was convicted. Elliott was threatened and shadowed by men who wanted to kill him and a few of the others.

Shortly after the trials ended, Joe Elliott went to South Dakota and was hired as a stock detective by the Western South Dakota Stock Growers Association and worked with Sam Moses. One case they worked led them to the northwest corner of Nebraska, where two rustlers were driving stolen cattle to an old stable and butchering them. When they snuck up on the two, one ran and the other pulled a .45 on Elliott but was too scared to use it. Another case took them to Deadwood, where a slaughterhouse burned the hides in a big furnace to eliminate the evidence. Elliott commented that "There were more thieves between the Black Hills and Pierre than there were cattlemen."

Like many stock detectives, Elliott was also a sworn deputy sheriff, reportedly in three counties at once. The threats of those who wanted to kill him for his activities in Wyoming never really slowed. What happened next has been told two entirely different ways. Joe Elliott told interviewer B. W. Hope, that he decided to just disappear and take up somewhere that he wasn't known. He said that he just left his horse and gear, took his Winchester, and walked out of the country. The hard way, no doubt. The other story is that he went back into Wyoming on a case and was caught by some of his many enemies who intended to kill him and made that thought plain to him. After some talking, they agreed to let Elliott go, on foot, with the warning not to ever set foot in Wyoming again. The road took him across the West, where he did some mining, served as a deputy sheriff in Plush, Oregon, and was the owner of an orchard, before settling in Boise, Idaho. He first met his wife at a boardinghouse there. Joe Elliott had indeed seen the elephant. He died April 17, 1946.

PHIL DUFRAN

Phil DuFran was born May 26, 1854, at Dubuque, Iowa. He was six years old when his family moved to Elk Point, Dakota Territory, in 1861. When still under twenty years of age, he was hired as a driver for a freighting train that ran between Yankton and Deadwood. He arrived in Deadwood on August 2, 1876, during one such trip. While resting in his wagon seat, he heard a gunshot from a saloon across the street and then saw a man run out of the establishment. Before he could land in the saddle, "men with guns drawn took hold of the man." He soon learned that it was James Butler "Wild Bill" Hickok who had been killed. DuFran later told how he and other men picked up Hickok's body and took him to be buried.

Phil DuFran next shows up on history's radar in a something less-than-auspicious manner. A small rancher in the west-central county of Custer, in Nebraska, DuFran was also a deputy sheriff. In 1878, Bob "Stevens" Olive, younger brother of "cattle king" Print Olive, discovered that homesteader Ami Ketchum had sold some Olive cattle at a Buffalo County stockyard. Luther Mitchell was implicated as well, since he and his family lived with Ketchum. Bob was deputized by Buffalo County sheriff Dave Anderson to arrest them. When confronted at their soddy, the suspected rustlers started shooting, which resulted in Bob's death. It was believed that a bullet from Mitchell's Winchester killed Bob Olive.

The accused rustlers were tracked down and arrested. The arresting sheriffs turned over the prisoners to Deputy Sheriff Phil DuFran, and Keith County sheriff Barney Gillan, who offered to help (and were probably interested in the reward) for transport back to Custer County, where the killing took place. The prisoners were DuFran's responsibility, as the crime occurred in his jurisdiction. Late one night during the trip, Print Olive and his cowboys intercepted the lawmen and offered the $750 reward in exchange for their prisoners. It appeared to be a sad showing for the two lawmen when they accepted the money and rode away. However contemptible their action seemed, the fact was, they had no choice. Even though, on occasion, Print Olive could be reasoned with, this would *not* have been one of those times. They knew the vengeful Olive would settle the score whether they accepted the reward or not. After the lawmen rode away, Olive and his men lynched Mitchell and Ketchum.

Phil DuFran led a full colorful life serving as a Nebraska deputy sheriff, Wyoming stock detective and Johnson County invader, businessman and South Dakota police chief. COURTESY AMERICAN HERITAGE CENTER, UNIVERSITY OF WYOMING

Within a couple of years, DuFran had moved to Wyoming and was employed by the Wyoming Stock Growers Association as a stock detective. In 1892, the big cattlemen, all WSGA members, were moving their army of gunslingers, ranch owners, foremen, and stock detectives north from Cheyenne. They planned to attack the "rustlers" of Johnson County at Buffalo. DuFran, was keeping an eye on things there, and when word reached the citizens of Buffalo that the WSGA invaders were on the way, they began to arm themselves. DuFran rode south with the news and met the invaders at the TA Ranch. They had already been told of Buffalo's response by another spy, but his details outlining the huge number of men involved convinced them to fortify at the TA Ranch.

When the Buffalo citizen army arrived at the TA Ranch, a battle ensued. Troops from Fort McKinney arrived at the TA, arrested them, and escorted them back to the fort. Phil DuFran was among those arrested. They were later transferred to Cheyenne where the case slogged through the courts without a single conviction.

Arizona soon became DuFran's next home, and he was hired by the Hashknife Ranch. He did finally return to South Dakota, where he was a representative for the Rosenbaum Brothers Commission House of Chicago. By 1909 he operated the Angel Saloon in LeBeau, an important railroad cattle shipping point. During the fall of 1909, over 150,000 head of cattle were shipped east. Most of them came from the nearby Matador ranch's five hundred thousand acres of Indian reservation land leased from the government.

Texas was the headquarters of the huge Matador Land and Cattle Company, which also had land in Montana and Canada. A principle owner was millionaire Murdo Mackenzie, past president of the National Livestock Association and friend of President Theodore Roosevelt. He assigned his son, David G. "Dode" Mackenzie, to the South Dakota ranch. In December 1909, the arrogant and sometimes troublesome Dode and other Matador cowboys rode into LeBeau. When they entered DuFran's saloon where Bud Stevens normally tended bar, the word was out that an armed Dode was hunting the bartender. Stevens had been fired from the Matador in Texas and didn't get along with Dode one little bit. Dode was belligerent, as usual, and one of the cowboys rode his horse into the saloon. When an argument started between the two, Stevens pulled out a .45 and shot Dode in the chest. As the wounded man stumbled to the door, Stevens shot him twice in the back.

There was no immediate reprisal for Dode's killing, but after Murdo came to the South Dakota ranch, he stopped shipping cattle through LeBeau. With no cattle to ship, the railroad moved out, sounding a death knell for the vibrant town.

Bud Stevens was acquitted in March 1910. Twenty months and one day later, a fire raged through LeBeau, destroying more than half of its buildings, including Phil DuFran's Angel Saloon. DuFran, who was then residing in Pierre, had $1,500 worth of insurance, but the loss was reported at $8,500. The insurance company reportedly adjusted the payout and DuFran rebuilt. Arson was thought to be the cause of the December 1, 1911, fire, in part because fire hoses had been cut and flammable chemicals had been found in the ruins. Today, the town is under the waters of the Oahe Reservoir.

Apparently a full-fledged businessman, DuFran took over management of the Grand Pacific Hotel in Pierre in July 1911. He planned to turn the hotel into a rooming house. By 1913, he was involved with Hughes County democratic politics as one of four majority electors and was in the saloon business in Pierre as well.

In December 1917, DuFran was hired as a wartime guard at the Milwaukee railroad's Missouri River bridge at Mobridge. The Pierre newspaper commented, "It will be a sorry day for the man who undertakes to tamper with the big $2,000,000 structure across the 'Big Muddy' with Phil DuFran doing sentry duty thereabout." Two weeks of subzero temperatures were too much for the sixty-year-old, however, so he resigned the position.

DuFran served as chief of police in Mobridge for six years during the 1920s but had to resign due to poor health. The memorable seventy-four-year life of Phil DuFran came to an end on April 23, 1929. He was buried in Mobridge.

SAMUEL NEAL "SAM" MOSES

Sam Moses was born in Washington County, Texas, about 1857. A tall Texan, he went north in 1878 as a trail hand driving a herd to Julesburg, Colorado. The next year he was a rider for the Sturgis and Goodell trail drive that ended in the Black Hills. He had worked on the TOT ranch and also was foreman of Whitcomb's Bar T Ranch. Moses was the first detective for the Fall River Protective Association, which had formed before the state organization. He ranched in the Bixby area, the Nebraska sandhills, Montana, Colorado, and lastly Custer County, South Dakota.

Moses was hired as the first WSDSGA detective on December 1, 1892, for a four-month period, at a monthly salary of $125 per month.

Although that was a good wage for the time, he was expected to furnish all necessary gear and pay his own expenses. If the need was absolute, he was allowed to hire extra help at $2.50 per day.

Apparently Moses didn't attend to his detective duties as quickly as the board desired, so at the association's executive committee meeting in February 1893, action was taken. A motion by Ed Lemmon was approved that canceled the contract with Moses and advised him that he would not be paid after January 15, 1893. This action got Moses's attention and he was rehired soon thereafter.

There could be little doubt, however, that Sam Moses was an effective stock detective, as indicated by five cattle thieves that he arrested. The five had posted bail, and while out of jail raised a $1,000 reward for the man who would kill Moses before they went to trial. Moses caught wind of this and promptly deposited all five back in jail, with a higher bond. During the first two years of his employment as a detective, he was able to achieve thirteen convictions, which was almost unheard of.

Many WSDSGA members also belonged to the Wyoming association, which helped inspect markets for South Dakota cattle. In the early 1890s, a committee was formed that directed the work of the detective-inspectors. The committee was made up of James Craig, F. M. Stewart, and Ed Lemmon. Craig had recommended that the association hire Joe Elliott as an additional stock detective, which was approved. Elliott had been one of the stock detectives who invaded Johnson County in 1892 on behalf of the big ranchers.

After the invaders were released from custody, Elliott relocated to South Dakota due to death threats made against him. While working a rustling case in Wyoming near Devil's Tower, Elliott came up missing and it was presumed that his enemies in that state had followed through on their threats.

In 1889 cowboy Ed Blakey was elected sheriff of Fall River County, South Dakota. He was good at fighting rustlers and appointed Moses deputy sheriff. (Blakey became a detective for the Western South Dakota Stock Growers Association in 1896.) They had been searching for "Spokane" Bill Augher, a suspected cattle thief. Luck was with them as they watched Spokane and a young man moving a small bunch of cattle.

Spokane shot a cow more than once with his six-shooter, until it fell. The two had started to skin the animal when Moses and Blakey made their approach. Moses ordered them to throw up their hands, but instead Spokane took cover behind the dead cow and fired on them. The two lawmen continued to advance, firing a Winchester and a Sharps rifle, perforating Spokane's cover. He thought better of his plan, tossed the pistol away, and stood up with hands raised. Spokane was convicted and sentenced to two and a half years in prison. Evidence that the association approved of Moses's part of the arrest and conviction of Spokane came in the form of a $125 bonus. The outlaw was released several months early for good behavior. While incarcerated, Spokane received patents for a bridle bit and a pair of stirrups.

Spokane had threatened Moses for his arrest, but when he got out of prison he moved to Montana. Ironically, he turned his life around and upon recommendation of a friend, was appointed as a stock detective. Spokane was killed while working in that capacity.

Respect for the work Moses had accomplished was shown by a short comment in the *Hot Springs Weekly Star*, on June 29, 1894: "Sam Moses and his partner Joe Elliott started out for some point in Custer Co. this morning pretty well armed and the STAR would not be surprised to hear of some cattle thief getting rounded up in pretty good shape."

The 1900 convention of the Western South Dakota Stock Growers Association was chiefly concerned with the rustling problem. Secretary Frank Stewart stated, "More cases of rustling have been reported in the past eight months than at any other time since this organization was formed." Members believed that the current prosperous range conditions were the reason for the increased thefts. At this time, WSDSGA detectives were Ed Blakey, William Hudspeth, William McCarthy, and Billy Moses (Butte County lawman, and brother to Sam). Billy later moved to Montana where he pinned on another badge and was killed performing his duties.

During Sam Moses's fascinating life not only was he a stock detective (sometimes held concurrently with other positions), he also served as sheriff of Fall River County, deputy US marshal, and a US Department of Justice special agent. One of the assignments he received from the Justice

The legendary South Dakota stock detective Sam Moses (right) with cattleman Ed "Dad" Lemmon at the stock growers Golden Anniversary convention in 1941 at Rapid City. COURTESY BERT HALL COLLECTION, STATE ARCHIVES, SOUTH DAKOTA HISTORICAL SOCIETY

Department was to track down the killers of slain deputy US marshal George Wellman, who was shot by rustlers in Wyoming. Moses tracked one of the gang throughout the Southwest for over three months, until finally arresting him in Indian territory and taking him back to Cheyenne. Sam Moses was honored for his contribution to the cattle industry by being included in the National Cowboy Hall of Fame. Moses died in 1943 and is buried in Belle Fourche, South Dakota.

OKLAHOMA "OKLA" NOONAN

Born in Ohio in 1843, John Smith Anderson labored in a sawmill as a young man. In 1861, he enlisted in the 13th Indiana Infantry Regiment that joined General George McClellan's troops. After mustering out three years later, Anderson returned to the sawmills. Health problems convinced him to try farming, so he made a move to Illinois, but the climate did nothing to ease his lung malady. His next stop was Texas. He found that working cattle suited him, but Union veterans weren't warmly received there, so he moved once again, this time near a sister in Kansas. Here Anderson met, courted, and married Lurena Lockhart. Their family's next home was Red River Station, Texas, where he once again found work as a drover. When news came that the government would be opening up the Indian and Oklahoma Territories to settlement, they moved to Arkansas City, Kansas, to await the official word. The Andersons were so convinced that Oklahoma would be their new home that they named their last daughter Oklahoma. "Okla" Anderson was born in 1884, but tragedy struck when Okla's mother soon passed away. Tired of waiting for the government's announcement and continued health problems, Anderson moved the family one last time, to Gila Bend, Arizona, where he established the Gila Land and Cattle Company. Okla learned how to rope and ride with the best, alongside her father in his successful venture. She married local cattleman Daniel W. Noonan Jr. in 1906.

A newspaper article appeared on July 9, 1915, that surely raised more than a few eyebrows. Arizona Livestock Sanitary Board secretary Sam Bradner announced the appointment of Mrs. Okla Noonan of Gila Bend as a state livestock inspector. Bradner explained that she had grown up in the saddle, was thoroughly familiar with the cattle business, was an expert at roping and tying steers, and was said to be the equal of any cowboy in the state. He went on to say, "Although she is the first woman in Arizona to be appointed to this position, if the experiment of the woman inspector proved successful, that it was possible that the board would name only women to this position."

The following month, a newspaper in Oklahoma ran an article titled, "Activities of Women—Interesting Notes of the Feminine Sex the World Over." Among brief notes of a woman barber in Philadelphia, women being trained as doctors in China, and female Austrian undertakers, was this one: "Arizona has a woman livestock inspector, probably the only one in the world, through the appointment of Mrs. Okla Noonan."

The "experiment" must have worked out, as Noonan was featured in the *Tombstone Epitaph* four years later. The 1919 article pointed out that Arizona claimed the distinction of having the only woman livestock inspector and detective in America.

Ed Stephens, Sanitary Board secretary at the time, pointed out that she held a most unusual position for a woman, and "the fact that she holds it [the position] well, is pretty solid proof of the fact that Arizona women can do anything the men can." He commented that on more than one occasion, Noonan caught rustlers red-handed and took them to a justice of the peace. Stephens explained that the woman livestock inspector's job was not an easy one. Their duties were to stop cattle rustling and check all shipments and brands. They had to spend many hours in the saddle, through all kinds of weather, wandering the cattle ranges, picking up mavericks, and looking into rumors of "brand manipulators." And, he said, they "must be possessed of cool bravery and good judgment, and most important, she must be handy with a six-gun, for true marksmanship is often called into play." These basic expectations were filed down a bit when he offered prospective women applicants some advice. Stephens suggested that "they spend some time every day in throwing small metal discs into the air and plugging them with a revolver bullet as they fall toward the earth. The applicant should also be experienced in the use of a rope at a gallop." He said that he was very proud of Mrs. Noonan and wished that he had more inspectors of either sex on his staff as efficient as she had proven to be.

It's unclear how many years Noonan served as a livestock inspector in Arizona. Oklahoma "Okla" Anderson Noonan passed away in 1950, at age sixty-five, six years after her husband, Daniel. The obituary explained that she had died in a Phoenix rest home after a long illness. She was not forgotten, as it noted that she was the first woman cattle inspector for the state sanitation board and a member of the Arizona Pioneers Association.

W. D. "DAVE" ALLISON

William Davis "Dave" Allison, born in Ohio in 1861, was a highly respected, longtime lawman. After arriving in Texas, he developed a fine reputation as a cowboy and horseman. He became known for having a cool head under pressure and was intelligent and well-liked by cattlemen.

Allison was so popular that he was nominated to run for Midland County sheriff. At only twenty-seven years old, he became the youngest sheriff in Texas at the time, when he won the election of 1888. He held the post for ten years. During his tenure, Allison applied for and received one of the Special Texas Ranger commissions that were allocated to the Cattle Raisers Association of Texas. The sheriff's notable record against stock thieves made this an easy appointment to obtain.

Allison's colorful career continued in 1899, when he was accepted into Company D, Texas Rangers, under Captain John R. Hughes. He later became city marshal of Roswell, New Mexico. In the spring of 1903, Allison was hired by Captain Thomas H. Rynning to serve as an Arizona Ranger. A proficient man-hunter, it appeared that Allison had one serious vice: gambling. Even though he rose through the ranks to ranger lieutenant, his vice caused his eventual dismissal. In 1883 he began working as an inspector for the Stock Raisers Association of Northwestern Texas, on an "as needed" basis. In 1917 he became a full-time inspector for the association.

In 1911, Horace L. "Hod" Roberson became an inspector and later worked with Allison, a close friend and associate. Roberson, a large man, had also been a ranger under Hughes, and fought in the Spanish-American War. He was also a cowboy and ranch foreman near the Mexican border. His toughness was never doubted.

Allison was appointed Special Texas Ranger for a second time, in 1917, to fight rustlers. Allison and Roberson were working together and after nearly a year of investigation, they obtained indictments on Milt Good and Tom Ross, among others, for cattle theft. They were scheduled to appear before a grand jury in Seminole on April 2, 1923, to present additional evidence against the suspects. On the evening before court, Allison and Roberson met with attorneys in the tiny lobby of the Gaines Hotel, where they were staying. A short time later Good and Ross pushed through the hotel doors and opened up with a shotgun and pistols, killing the two inspectors. Mrs. Roberson, upstairs in her room, heard the shots and ran down to the lobby, where she saw

Longtime lawman Dave Allison was shot to death along with inspector partner Horace Roberson in the lobby of the Gaines Hotel in Seminole, Texas, by suspected rustlers. COURTESY BOB ALEXANDER, *FEARLESS DAVE ALLISON: BORDER LAWMAN*

her bloody, lifeless husband in a chair, and the body of Dave Allison on the floor. The killers were just walking through the doors to leave when she grabbed her dead husband's .45. The grips had been damaged by bullets so she retrieved his extra gun, a Colt .25 automatic pistol, from his belt. She stepped outside of the hotel and opened up on the killers, guns still in hand, hitting Ross in the stomach and another round penetrating Good's arm and lodging in his hip. The wounds were not immediately life threatening, but serious enough that they required professional medical treatment. Due to their condition, they shortly afterwards turned themselves in, were convicted and sent to prison. Not down for long, a couple of years later both escaped. Ross was eventually located in Montana, where he killed a man and then committed suicide. Good was captured and served more time in Huntsville. He was paroled finally, only to be crushed to death between a pasture gate and his own car near Cotulla, Texas, in 1960.

JOHN R. BANISTER

During the late 1870s, young John Banister was a cowboy for the Joe Franks outfit in Texas. By 1877 Banister was sworn in as a member of Lieutenant N. O. Reynolds's newly re-formed Company E, Texas Rangers, which was stationed at Lampasas. A close brush with death came the following year when Banister was in a detachment of Company E, looking for Indians who had been stealing horses. The detachment had bedded down for the night and Banister had pulled first watch. Around midnight, one of the pack mules became agitated over something in the brush behind him. John walked slowly to the area, Winchester in hand, when not more than ten feet away, an Indian jumped up and fired at him. The bullet whizzed dangerously by. He fired back as the Indian ran. The camp was awakened by the first shot and joined Banister in the chase. Many shots were fired at the Indian, but he was able to make good his escape.

In July 1878 Banister was one of the rangers in the last fight with the notorious outlaw Sam Bass. The outlaw died from a bullet wound received in the fight with Texas Rangers at Round Rock, Texas. With the resignation of Lieutenant Reynolds, Banister transferred to Company B under Captain Marsh.

In 1881 he left the rangers and worked cattle drives into Kansas. He had six children with his first wife, who died in 1892, and five with his second. From about 1889 to 1892, Banister served as a detective for the Santa Fe railroad and others. He then spent six years as a US Treasury agent on the Mexican border to police cattle smugglers.

By 1898 Banister became a field inspector for the Cattle Raisers Association of Texas (CRAT). His earlier experience as a ranger and detective made him an effective officer. He became chief of the association's Field Inspection Service, which he established and which still operates today. In September of that year, he was sent to Pawhuska, Oklahoma, to investigate cattle thefts from an association member there. CRAT had many members in other states and inspectors would work on their livestock theft cases as well. After talking to member Albert Appel about the theft, he located a fellow inspector in the area and the two proceeded to John Rippie's ranch near Foraker. They talked to Rippie about his cattle, but the nervous rancher said he couldn't show them to the inspectors until the next day. Deciding not to wait, Banister and his fellow inspector rode to Rippie's pasture. There they observed several head of cattle with altered brands. They noted what they saw and the next day met again with the rancher, who agreed to ride out to his herd with them. Banister asked him if the cattle all belonged to him. Incredulously, he said they did. After closer inspection, Banister informed Rippie that he was claiming a half dozen cattle for their rightful owners and proceeded to name them. Rippie didn't object. The next day Banister presented his evidence to the county attorney at Pawhuska, who agreed to issue an arrest warrant for John Rippie. Banister and another inspector arrested the rancher and took him to appear before district court. Rippie was one of many cattle thieves arrested during Bannister's service with the association.

Texas cattle inspector John Banister (right) points out a blotted brand in Oklahoma.
COURTESY TEXAS & SOUTHWESTERN CATTLE RAISERS FOUNDATION/MUSEUM, FORT WORTH, TEXAS

John R. Banister was serving as sheriff of Coleman County, Texas, when he died of a stroke in 1918, which ended his forty-two-year career as a lawman. His wife, Emma (Daugherty), filled out her husband's remaining term and is recognized as the first female sheriff in America.

FRANK R. LEVIGNE

Frank Levigne was known as a professional lawman. He held several positions, including Pinkerton operative, railroad special agent, police detective, deputy sheriff, and chief livestock inspector in the early twentieth century. Levigne was born in Memphis, Tennessee, on November 29, 1866. By his eighteenth birthday, he had traveled through Montana and settled in Spokane, Washington Territory. By 1904, he became operative 15 of the famed Pinkerton National Detective Agency. He worked many kinds of criminal cases, from safe blowing to infiltration of the Industrial Workers of the World (IWW), and covered several western states besides Washington.

Rustling continued to hinder progress for Montana stockmen. Even though a state association existed, frustrated ranchers formed the Northern Montana Roundup Association (NMRA) in 1895. By the turn of the century, thousands of people had settled in Montana. By this time, cattle rustling involved a network of people from the rustlers themselves to butchers, shippers, and others less conspicuous. It became much more difficult to track down those responsible because of this coordinated system.

By 1910 Thomas C. Power, one of the largest ranchers in the region, was fed up with the financial problems and the inefficiency of the state's inspectors. The number of inspector-detectives had been reduced from thirty-four in 1905 to seven in 1910. D. W. Raymond, secretary of the board of stock commissioners, admitted to problems when he stated, "Detective work is not as effective as it might be."

In April 1910, Power notified the Pinkerton's Spokane office of his desire to hire a detective to investigate cattle theft and butchering near his ranches. The lack of success forced Power to fire the first Pinkerton, operative 9, after his secret business was discovered by mailing in his reports from the local post office. Operative 83, hired in early 1914, who was able to gain only a small amount of information but made no arrests.

Another operative, Frank Levigne, went to work in the Conrad area. After a few months of tedious interviews and investigation, Levigne, "Porky" Sellers, a local inspector, and Teton County attorney D. W. Doyle were able to charge and convict Edward Regan and W. L. Schroder of cattle theft. The thieves each received one year in prison. Doyle wrote to Levigne's chief in Spokane, stating, "The suspects had covered up their trail beyond detection, making the case an unusually hard one. There was never a man more on the job than Mr. Levigne, he was absolutely untiring in his efforts to secure evidence and to render every assistance to the prosecution."

For the year 1914, Thomas Power paid the Pinkerton agency $1,300. Even as these two men went to prison, reports of more stolen stock came in and Levigne began a new investigation. The next year, he accepted the appointment as chief detective for the Montana Board of Stock Commissioners, a post he held until 1925. Levigne found love in Great Falls, marrying Mary Zoe Capron in December 1920. The wedding was attended by the bride's two sons, one from Denver and one from Philadelphia. They resided in Helena. The newspaper announcement included the comment, "Mr. Levigne is very well known over Montana having been in charge of the work of prevention and detection of livestock thefts for several years." Between 1925 and 1928, he joined the Alberta (Canada) Provincial Police, and served as a Lewis and Clark County deputy sheriff. He worked the last three years of his career as a detective with the Edmonton (Canada) Police, retiring in 1931, at age sixty-five.

EMORY E. CLARK

Emory Clark was born November 22, 1883, on a ranch near Pueblo, Colorado. He worked as a cowboy on the family ranch until he was twenty-four years old. In 1907, he pinned on a Routt County deputy sheriff's badge. He eventually worked up to undersheriff and was then elected sheriff. After his term was up, he moved his family to Denver. During World War I, he served as chairman of the Routt County Draft Board, and organized and sought volunteers for the First Colorado Cavalry.

In 1920, Clark moved to North Platte, Nebraska, this time to accept a position with the Nebraska Stock Growers Association (NSGA) as an inspector with the cattle theft investigation department. During his long tenure, he served as chief of the theft department, and in 1941, when livestock enforcement duties were taken over by the newly formed Nebraska Brand Committee (NBC), Clark was chief investigator and assistant chief inspector. The office of state sheriff was established by state statute in 1927, and he was commissioned as a state deputy sheriff. This law is what gave stock inspectors for the NSGA, and later the NBC investigators, statewide police powers.

To see what the daily work of an inspector looked like in the 1920s, here are excerpts from Clark's reports to the NSGA during September and October 1923:

On the 10th I went to Bridgeport for the purpose of determining conditions generally in this part of the country. On my arrival in Bridgeport I met with Sheriff Davis and made an appointment for the following day.

. . . On the 11th I met with the sheriff and held a conference with him relative to matters which had recently come up in the district regarding the disappearance of cattle. The sheriff informed me that he had information that a man by the name of B— who lived in the vicinity of Bridgeport for some time but who left the country last spring had returned. The sheriff stated further that he believed this man B— was implicated in the stealing of a bunch of cattle from a man by the name of L— and also from J—. These men live near Bayard and their cattle which were stolen were unbranded. From information given me by the Sheriff I have reason to believe that a crook named N— was implicated in the stealing of these cattle. I requested that the sheriff take this man into custody and give me an opportunity to drill him but it seems that the sheriff was unable to locate this man during my stay in Bridgeport. He assured me however that he would try to pick this man up later and that he would work with me a few days in the vicinity of Bridgeport on cattle cases. I was further informed by the sheriff that there were a number of cattle in the B— pasture bearing various brands at this time not

known to the sheriff. On further investigation I found that these cattle were New Mexico cattle being pastured and that B— had nothing whatever to do with them.

. . . On the 14th I went to Bayard to the Mong ranch where I interviewed Mr. Mong and investigated further loss of Mong cattle. It seemed to be the general opinion of the community that these cattle might have gone toward Running Water. Have had a good deal of information that the cattle had been trailed back and forth between river points and points on the Running Water. I decided to make a trip across this country and look through pastures enroute, and also pastures located on the Running Water. During the evening I got in touch with the manager of the sales ring and was informed by him that no cattle had been sold at that point so far this year.

. . . The 24th was spent in court, during the day H— was taken into court and pled guilty to the charge of stealing 38 head of cattle from the R— pasture.

. . . October 17th at Sterling I met George Watson who is manager of the American Cattle Company. Mr. Watson informed me that his company had recovered some of the cattle stolen from them out of South Dak. last spring. These cattle were found near Platte, South Dak. Mr. Watson further stated that they had found forty eight hides with worked over brands in the B— Packing House at Sioux City. He further stated that he had warned the Inspector at that point to watch for these cattle, but they had gone by the Inspector, sold to the packers and butchered. These cattle were stolen by a man name of S— who has been making his headquarters near Platte, South Dakota, the past year or two. A warrant was obtained for the arrest of this man, but he escaped when the sheriff tried to arrest him, and is still at large. Mr. Watson further informed me that he has reason to believe that there is a lot of crooked work going on near Platte, and I believe it would be a good idea to look this Country over when cattle begin to go in on feed lots there.

. . . The 21st was spent in Alliance, and during the Night I was called by the Sheriff to look for some stolen Horses in the Alliance Stockyards, on information from the Sheriff at Gillette, Wyoming. I worked most of the night in the Yards, examining these horses carefully, and finally finding the two horses that had been described by the Sheriff at Gillette. One of these horses was a black horse, branded "42" left shoulder. The other a bay horse branded "3" left jaw. After finding these horses, I went with the Sheriff to the Alliance Hotel, where we arrested G— and L— who were in charge of these horses from Gillette to Ft. Worth, Texas.

Accompanying each monthly report of Clark's was a list of expenses incurred in carrying out his duties:

Oct.	*1st*	*Room Rent*	*$16.00*
	1st	*Meals*	*2.75*
	1st	*Telephone*	*.80*
	2nd	*Meals*	*2.50*
	2nd	*Telephone calls*	*.75*
	3rd	*Gas and oil*	*2.10*
	3rd	*Meals*	*1.50*
	4th	*Gas and oil*	*1.30*

Emory Clark retired in 1955, closing out a forty-eight-year law-enforcement career. He moved his family to Fowler, Colorado, where he died on January 22, 1958.

FRANK M. CANTON

Arguably, no other stock detective in Wyoming had a more sketchy past than that of Joe Horner, alias Frank Canton. For sure, he was not the only cowboy to come up from Texas in the dust of a longhorn cattle drive, and certainly not the only one evading Texas authorities by doing so. Canton, however, had been an inmate of the state prison at Huntsville until he decided to take his leave. The convictions for bank and stagecoach robberies would apparently use up too much of his time.

Escaped Texas prison inmate Joe Horner, alias Frank Canton, became well known as a Wyoming lawman, stock detective and member of the Johnson County invaders. COURTESY AMERICAN HERITAGE CENTER, UNIVERSITY OF WYOMING

He accepted a job with the Wyoming Stock Growers Association (WSGA) as a stock detective in 1880 and was stationed in Johnson County. Two years later the convict was elected sheriff, and later won reelection. In 1888, the popular Red Angus defeated Canton for the office. Canton then returned to work as an association stock detective when hard feelings began to fester between the big cattlemen and the "encroaching" settlers, who had the audacity to start their own small herds. Prominent members of the WSGA finally decided to eliminate those deemed by them to be rustlers, sans benefit of a trial. These men formed an assassination squad, whose members were stock detectives Frank Canton, Deputy Sheriff Fred Coates, Billy Lykens, Joe Elliott, and occasionally Mike Shonsey, private stock detective and ranch foreman. In the summer of 1891, three masked men took horse rancher and accused thief Tom Waggoner and lynched him. No one was ever charged with the murder, but word was that the three prime suspects were stock detectives Joe Elliott, Thomas Smith, and Deputy Sheriff Fred Coates. This hadn't been the first murder. A war between large cattle interests and the homesteaders in Johnson County, Wyoming, was eminent. The assassins attacked the tiny cabin where blacklisted cattlemen Nate Champion and Ross Gilbertson were staying, and a gunfight ensued. The attackers retreated. They were identified as Canton, Elliott, and Lykens with help from Shonsey. Later, another attack on Champion and his new partner, Nick Ray, at their KC cabin, resulted in their deaths. The culmination of the "war" was the armed invasion of Johnson County by the association's hired-gun army. The invaders were finally arrested by the US Army at the KC Ranch. Among the forty-plus "invaders" who were arrested were Frank Canton, Joe Elliott, Ben Morrison, and Mike Shonsey. None were ever convicted.

The amazing career of escaped convict Joe Horner (Canton) continued. Before his death in 1927, he served as a packinghouse manager in Nebraska, deputy US marshal in Oklahoma and Alaska, bounty hunter, and was appointed as Oklahoma's first adjutant-general in 1907.

MIKE SHONSEY

When Mike Shonsey died, he was known as the last surviving participant of the infamous 1892 invasion of Johnson County, Wyoming, known as the Johnson County War. He worked during that time as a ranch foreman and livestock detective.

Shonsey was born to Irish parents, Thomas and Margaret (McCarthy) Shonsey, in Montreal, Canada, on September 6, 1866. The family moved to Caledonia, Ohio, when Shonsey was five. When Thomas was killed in a lumbering accident, the four Shonsey boys became responsible for the family's income.

It was in Ohio where Mike met a man who would shape his life and livelihood. Thomas Benton "T. B." Hord was a farmer and successful sheepman who desired to expand into the western range cattle industry. After moving to Cheyenne in 1880, Hord became involved in local affairs and was an organizer of the town's first bank, Citizens National. He formed a partnership with fellow Ohio natives William E. and S. A. Guthrie, under the name of Guthrie, Hord & Co. Hord expanded his own business interests, so in 1884 the partnership dissolved. He had employed twelve-year-old Shonsey as a wrangler until August 1884, when he sent the young man to Central City, Nebraska, to work at the new cattle feeding operation of which Hord was a partner. By 1886, Hord had incorporated with other investors and formed the Lance Creek Cattle Company, with headquarters at the 77 Ranch near Lusk, Wyoming. The 77 brand belonged to W. C. Lykens, who transferred it to D. B. Wyatt, who sold it to Hord.

In the late 1880s, Shonsey worked for other cattle interests as well, including the Carey C. Y. at Casper, the E. K. outfit of the Western Union Beef Company, and W. E. Guthrie, an executive committee member of the Wyoming Stock Growers Association.

Shonsey married Olive Belle Sisler in O'Neill, Nebraska, January 14, 1891. In just over a year, Mike would be searching for rustlers as the Wyoming Stock Growers Association's army of gunmen started north from Cheyenne. His position was strictly pro–big cattle interests. Frank

Wyoming/Nebraska cowboy and stock detective Mike Shonsey, was the last surviving participant of the Johnson County War when he died in 1954. He is shown here in Wyoming wearing his Colt Single-Action Army in a Mexican loop holster and ammo belt for his Winchester Model 1886 carbine. COURTESY AMERICAN HERITAGE CENTER, UNIVERSITY OF WYOMING

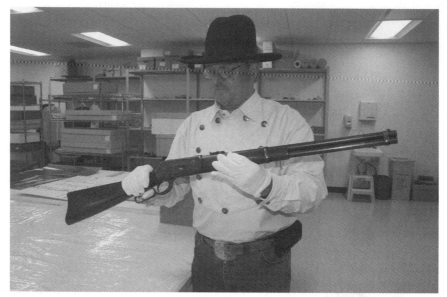

The author examining Mike Shonsey's Winchester Model 1886 carbine in .38-56 caliber, at the Nebraska History Museum. Donated to the museum by the family, this is the carbine held by Mike Shonsey in the photo on the previous page. COURTESY ANN MCCORD

Canton engaged Shonsey to work as a stock detective to reconnoiter ahead of the invading army of "regulators" and report current locations and numbers of those blacklisted by the WSGA. They were the regulator's targets. Canton was ex-chief of the WSGA Detective Bureau, but he was in charge of those stock detectives who were members of the invading army. Their destination was Johnson County, which was believed to be the nest for the worst livestock thieves.

Shonsey had been part of the group that attacked the cabin of Nate Champion and then-partner Ross Gilbertson. Later, at gunpoint, Champion forced Shonsey to name the other attackers, which he did.

Shonsey met up with the invaders and informed them that rustlers were holed up in a cabin at the KC Ranch. Some of the men wanted to continue toward Buffalo, but they were outvoted. The next attack came at the KC cabin of Nate Champion and Nick Ray. This time Champion and new partner Ray were killed in a hail of bullets.

Word was received that about two hundred citizens of the county had armed themselves at Buffalo, so the invading army of gunmen took refuge at the TA Ranch. After a prolonged gun battle, the US Army arrived. Mike Shonsey was among those arrested. After the prosecution of the invaders fizzled out, Shonsey returned to work as foreman of the 77 Ranch for the Lance Creek Cattle Company.

In later years, W. E. Guthrie said of Shonsey, "[Shonsey] became a key man, assigned in addition to his regular work, to gathering information to funnel to the cattle interests . . . he proved adept at this activity, confirming rustling and other illegal actions underway."

Russell Thorp, WSGA executive secretary/chief inspector (1930– 1949), explained about his good friend Mike Shonsey, in regards to the Johnson County invasion, "Throughout his life, Mike was a 'law and order' man. This being his disposition, and his employer, [George] Baxter, being one of the prime movers in the 'Invasion,' it was inevitable that Shonsey would become involved." Thorp said that he asked Shonsey directly why he joined the invasion, since he was an "employee." Shonsey replied that he had "ridden the range for years and had seen all kinds of rustling . . . all the way from dry-gulching the cows to stealing their unbranded calves, cutting brands out of the hides of live animals, running cattle off to isolated places to get the mavericks six-months and over—and I could not stand to witness those depredations at the expense of [my] employers." Regarding the common question of whether the accused rustlers were really rustlers, Shonsey explained, "The cattlemen were accused of being ruthless and of charging innocent men with stealing cattle, when as a matter of fact, every man on the [WSGA] blackball list was known without question of doubt to be a rustler. They were very particular in this regard."

On May 23, 1893, Shonsey, noticing a northbound cattle herd camped on the 77 range, rode out to ask the trail boss how long they would be there. Dave Matthews, trail foreman, rode out to meet him. Following behind Matthews was Dud Champion, brother of the slain Nate, who had stopped into the trail outfit's camp. Champion rode up as Shonsey and Matthews talked. The *Cheyenne Leader* of May 26, 1893, described the incident:

A Few More Details

Champion came up and did not appear to recognize Shonsey at first, but in a few minutes said, "Hello Mike." Shonsey said, "Hello Dud. I understand you threatened to kill me on first sight?" at the same time drawing his gun. Champion said, "No, hold up," and Shonsey lowered his pistol. Champion then reached for his gun and got it out, when Shonsey shot and Champion fell from his horse. He struck on the ground on the right side of his face. Shonsey fired two more shots at Champion before he moved, and then Champion tried to shoot Shonsey but could not cock the gun. Shonsey fired another shot at Champion and then rode off.

Matthews, who didn't know Shonsey or Champion previously, stayed with Dud. He asked why he didn't shoot back. Dud kept repeating, "I can't cock it! I can't cock it." Before Champion died about ten minutes later, he handed Matthews his pistol and said, "Take my six-shooter and tell the boys Mike Shonsey killed me." When Champion's body was retrieved, it was discovered that his revolver was too dirt packed to function.

At the inquest, Matthews and three of his men testified that at their camp, they all heard Dud Champion threatening to kill Mike Shonsey on sight. The judgment of the coroner's jury was self-defense. When asked by Russell Thorp to recount for him the killing of Dud Champion, Shonsey said he had heard that Dud was out to kill him for revenge. Champion believed that Shonsey killed his brother Nate at the KC Ranch, which Shonsey denied to Thorp. On the day Dud was killed, Shonsey said he was out checking on a Texas trail herd going north. "[Shonsey] looked up and saw a man riding down the Horseshoe toward him, about four o'clock in the afternoon ... the rider pulled his hat down, and then a second time, and I became suspicious." Shonsey said he pulled his six-shooter out and stuck it into his pants for a free draw. When Shonsey recognized Dud Champion, he said, "Hello, I understand you are out to kill me on sight." Champion replied that it was a lie and at the same time drew his gun, but Shonsey's gun fired first. The bullet knocked Champion out of the saddle onto his back, with his head pointing to Shonsey. Champion held the gun in both hands over his head aiming toward Shonsey, who shot him a second time. Shonsey said that he rode back to the 77 Ranch to change horses and clothes. That night he rode sixty miles to Douglas, Wyoming, where he gave himself up to Deputy Sheriff Harve Allen.

Even though Mike Shonsey was indeed a man who could take care of himself, he also had his wife, Olive Belle, to consider. When T. B. Hord again extended a job offer to Shonsey shortly after the Dud Champion shooting, they packed up and moved to Central City, Nebraska. The Shonseys started a family with the birth of John in 1894, followed by Michael G. in 1897, and Thomas in 1899.

Hord transferred Shonsey to nearby Clarks in 1898 to manage his growing feeder operations there. Shonsey was an effective and hard-working manager for his longtime friend. By 1903, *Nebraska Resources Illustrated* declared that Hord's Central City feeding operation was the largest in the United States.

Tragedy struck on November 11, 1905 when thirty-nine-year-old Olive Belle passed away at St. Joseph's Hospital in Omaha, after a long illness. The following year, Shonsey married Hannah L. Harris in Columbus, Nebraska. This was also the year that Shonsey bought out T. B. Hord's partner. The new company became the Hord and Shonsey Cattle Company. When Hord passed away in 1910, the enterprises included twenty Nebraska ranches covering twenty thousand acres, fifty grain elevators, and numerous feedlots located along three different rail lines. These livestock entities handled ten thousand cattle, ten thousand sheep, and seven thousand hogs per year.

Hord's death left open the board president's seat. In January 1911, Mike Shonsey was voted in as president and Hord's son, Heber, was elected vice-president. Shonsey became active in civic affairs, including helping to organize the Mid-State Irrigation District and becoming president of the Lincoln Highway Association, not to mention his three world steer-roping championships.

Not until the agricultural decline began in the 1920s did profits suffer for the hugely successful company. The Depression years were devastating, however, and the Hord and Shonsey Cattle Company ceased operations in 1942. Other Hord businesses continued on into the 1970s.

Mike Shonsey died at a Council Bluffs, Iowa, hospital on August 5, 1954 at age eighty-seven. The *Lincoln Star* read, "Death Claims Michael Shonsey, Last Survivor of Wyoming War." He was buried at the Central City, Nebraska, cemetery. Interestingly, Mike Shonsey Jr. was an inspector for the Wyoming Stock Growers Association in 1936.

JAMES T. WEBB

James Webb was appointed stock inspector by the Montana livestock commission in May 1902, replacing John W. Collins, who had resigned. His district of responsibility was Yellowstone and Sweet Grass Counties. The announcement of his appointment indicated that Webb, born in Missouri, was known as an old-time cowboy from Colorado who had worked for many large ranches there and in Montana.

A diligent inspector, Webb stayed busy. One of his 1903 cases involved filing a complaint against a Billings butcher for failing to comply with the law requiring monthly reports of the number of cattle butchered and the brands thereof. He tracked horse thieves too, and was reported on one occasion to have been on the trail with Undersheriff Thomas Sayles, searching for a man who stole a horse in town. He arrested another man for selling beef without exhibiting the hide to the buyer.

The following year Webb pursued Lee Chatwood and R. H. Williver for stealing a valuable mare. The relentless stock inspector arrested both men and took them to jail. In June, Webb was a passenger on the Northern Pacific train that derailed at Rapids. Even though his seat was torn loose from the floor, he wasn't injured.

James Webb was part of a posse that tracked down Oliver C. Mosier, one of two men wanted for holding up the Owl saloon in Billings and killing a police sergeant. Just after midnight on July 2, 1904, Mosier and Ed Grady entered the saloon known for its gambling operations. Even though both men wore masks, everyone in the saloon knew the local men. After gathering up some two hundred dollars, they exited through the back door. They didn't know that a man in the back room had overheard their demands and slipped out to summon police. As the two stepped out of the saloon, Sergeant Robert J. Hanna approached them in the alley. The two men opened fire, one with a shotgun, the other emptying his pistol into Hanna, killing him instantly. Stock Inspector Webb, Yellowstone County undersheriff Thomas Sayles, and Carbon County sheriff Potter tracked Mosier over ninety-five miles into Wyoming, where they made the arrest.

A week later, Melissa J. Merrill, a friend of Ed Grady, confirmed that the $750 reward would be paid if her information led to the capture of Grady. Once assurances were given her, Merrill sent for Webb, whom she knew well and trusted. A meeting was set up at 10 p.m., near the canal bridge of Twenty-Ninth Street in Billings. Other officers were posted a short distance away and waited. The meeting went afoul when passersby crossed the bridge, which spooked Grady, and he ran into the darkness. The lawmen decided not to wait another night, now knowing the vicinity where Grady was hiding out. They surrounded the area and began their search. When taken by surprise, Grady tried to act like he was working on the canal project. One of the officers close by recognized him, however, and he was taken into custody. Both Mosier and Grady confessed to the robbery and the killing of Police Sergeant Hanna. Mosier gave the location of the masks and pump shotgun that they had thrown into a ditch.

In early September 1904, James Webb arrested two brothers, Silas and Robert Parkinson, when he caught them driving forty-nine mares and colts. All of the horses' brands had been changed or completely blotted out. They were also charged with burglarizing a sheepman's house on Blue Creek. After lodging the Parkinsons in the county jail, Webb began the chore of deciphering the brands.

Late on Friday, September 23, 1904, ten prisoners escaped from the Yellowstone County jail, including murderers Ed Grady and Oliver Mosier, along with the Parkinson brothers. Webb and other officers set out to track down the others. Within a week, all but the above-mentioned four prisoners had been recaptured. On October 1, a message was received from Stock Detective Webb, who had caught the Parkinson brothers in Parkman, Wyoming, and was on his way back with them. Mosier and Grady remained at large.

On another case in March 1905, Inspector Webb's investigation lead him to recover five horses at Moorcroft, Wyoming. The horses had been stolen from C. O. Gruwell of Dawson County, Montana.

James Webb proved to be a relentless stock detective in Montana when appointed in 1902. He served a little over a year as Yellowstone County sheriff when he was killed in 1908 while arresting a horse thief. REPRINTED WITH PERMISSION FROM THE NATIONAL LAW ENFORCEMENT OFFICERS MEMORIAL

In January 1907 James Webb assumed the office of Yellowstone County sheriff. It was a position for which he had neither solicited nor campaigned—that was all done by his supporters—but which he nevertheless accepted. His notoriety as a resolute stock inspector had won him much respect and the election over the popular incumbent W. P. Adams.

Sheriff Webb set out to capture horse thief William Bickford, who was wanted at Worland, Wyoming. He located the man on March 24, 1908, about fifty miles north of Billings on the Woolfolk and Richardson sheep ranch. Accompanied by ranch co-owner James Richardson, they went to the sheep wagon where employee Bickford was resting. Sheriff Webb entered the wagon and asked Bickford where he was from. When he replied, "Wyoming," Webb picked up the man's revolver and told him he was arresting him.

According to Richardson, they stepped out of the wagon and talked further. Bickford quickly retrieved his Winchester from the wagon and ordered the sheriff to hold up his hands. Webb made a joke, apparently not believing Bickford was serious. The thief fired at Webb's feet and repeated his order. Webb started to back away, now realizing the gravity of the situation. Bickford fired again, sending a bullet into Webb's chest, killing him instantly. He took back his revolver, noticed that Richardson looked fearful, and said that he wouldn't hurt him.

A large posse of cowboys took the trail to find Bickford. At least one newspaper report commented that, "It is the opinion of most every man here that if Bickford is caught there will not be any court trial." The forty-year-old Webb had served as sheriff for only one year and three months.

The day after Webb's murder, Deputy Sheriff Taylor and lawyer Jack Herford spotted Bickford in the foothills of the Snowy Mountains, in the Musselshell. The killer quickly jumped into a camp wagon and started firing at the two-man posse. The officers opened up on the wagon. After many shots were exchanged, they heard one shot from inside the wagon. They carefully approached and found Bickford dead of a gunshot wound in the temple. He was buried nearby, but after receiving orders from Billings, his remains were taken there, where he was buried in potter's field.

The shock of the murder reverberated throughout Yellowstone County. Sheriff James Webb had been a truly revered lawman. An editorial in the *Billings Gazette* of March 27, 1908, read in part, ". . . robbed Yellowstone County of a most efficient public official and closed the career of one of the most fearless criminal hunters in the west."

It was learned from a close associate of Bickford that Bickford had admitted to the nighttime ambush murder of the Park County sheriff in 1899. The case had remained unsolved ever since.

Sheriff James T. Webb's funeral, administered by the Yellowstone County Bar Association, was held on March 30, inside the Coliseum rink in Billings. It was estimated that between 2,200 and 2,500 friends and supporters were seated in the auditorium, with as many standing outside. Webb had been a man of few words, had few if any intimate friends, and no confidants. His brother, F. M. Webb of Oregon, the only immediate relative, attended the services that were officiated by Reverend Samuel Fritsch, of the Congregational Church. With services concluded, the six pallbearers, all sheriffs from Montana and Wyoming, loaded the coffin into the hearse. The procession headed to Mountview Cemetery with Webb's horse "Baldy" being led by a deputy sheriff directly behind the hearse. The empty saddle was decorated with white roses.

Attorney O. F. Goddard, in his eloquent eulogy said in part, "You could not love such a man, but you were forced to admire and respect him, and would risk your all for him. Such men are scarce and their worth is not to be measured by the ordinary rules by which a man's worth is calculated."

On Decoration Day, May 31, 1909, the local Grand Army of the Republic (GAR) post organized a parade to the cemetery where school-children would decorate the graves of departed soldiers. In addition to the usual ritual of the order, they featured another observance, the unveiling of the Sheriff James Webb memorial in the courthouse yard. The memorial was a public drinking fountain made of Vermont granite that bore the late sheriff's name and paid for by public donations. The county attorney delivered a eulogy at the unveiling, noting that it was the first time in the county's history that a memorial was dedicated to one of her departed citizens. In describing Webb, he finished with, "Of uniform good nature, generous to his own detriment, of unimpeachable and unquestioned integrity, of the most exemplary habits, his private life was without a stain, and his every act and deed above reproach."

CHAPTER 6

The Anti-Horse Thief Association

THE IMAGE OF A RIOTOUS, TORCH-CARRYING THRONG MARCHING TOWARD the local hoosegow, preparing to administer "vigilante justice," has been indelibly etched in our minds, thanks to Hollywood. These events did, unfortunately, happen in the Old West and the early twentieth century. Some locales organized local vigilance committees that would assemble when needed to assist local lawmen. Sadly, these groups would occasionally get out of control and dispense prairie justice in the middle of nowhere. Getting caught with someone else's horse or moving a few cows with another's brand would qualify the unlucky person for a prairie hearing. Carrying out "justice" where there was no local law, or because local law was *thought* to be incompetent, was the justification of vigilantes.

A vigilance organization called "The Club," provided the first sort of law enforcement for the young town of Plattsmouth in the mid-1850s. The Nebraska Territory was formed in 1854, which lessened the duties of the group as territorial lawmen were appointed. In 1855, The Club merged into what was called "The Vigilantes Band," whose activities were then aimed primarily at claim jumpers and horse theft, two of the most serious offenses one could commit besides murder. The vigilantes conducted their own extralegal trials, and those prisoners found guilty were executed. Less severe punishment was usually given by a legal court of law, which made the vigilantes more desirous of holding trials themselves. To illustrate their zeal in battling criminals, on at least one occasion, several claim jumpers were found guilty by the group. With hands and feet tied, the prisoners were loaded into a rowboat for transport across the Missouri River to Iowa, for the purpose of banishment from Nebraska Territory. Upon the return of the vigilantes, they reported that due to an accident halfway across the river, all prisoners had been lost.

In 1864 Andy Taylor, territorial sheriff of Cass County, Nebraska, was aided in the capture of three horse thieves by the vigilantes. The group headed back to Plattsmouth, the county seat, with their prisoners and at nightfall they got permission from a local farmer to spend the night at his house. The next day, the "posse" headed out, stopping at Eight Mile Grove. The vigilantes decided that they would try the prisoners themselves and put forth an impressive day-long trial before the three were hung simultaneously from a tree branch. They were buried in a common grave. One of the condemned men was allowed to write a note to his mother, which he asked to be read aloud after he was hung, before sending it along to her. The tersely written note said:

> Dear Mother, Our mischief for the past few years has come to an end. We got to stretch rope. Don't grieve, mother, meet us in heaven.

It is presumed that Sheriff Taylor was present. What part, if any, he played in this incident isn't known. The vigilante group disbanded in 1865 because thieves found it too dangerous to operate in the area. It was stated by those who felt the vigilantes' actions were justified that "Unless the settlers used drastic measures in dealing with claim jumpers and horse thieves, they might as well give up their claims and their visions of independent, happy homes in the west and return to the east from whence they came."

An eloquent account of these three horse thieves and lynch law was recorded in papers of the Nebraska State Historical Society (NSHS) in 1887, and included the following:

> I think no well-informed and dispassionate person will dispute the proposition that a community will prosper in all their surroundings only as it enacts and faithfully executes good and wholesome laws. . . . The peculiar circumstances attending the stealing of horses and the facilities for the escape of the thief, on the borders of new settlements, has indicated

the class of horse thieves as one demanding sure and speedy extinction. From hasty action under this feeling probably many innocent men have suffered, while a much larger number, taken red-handed in the act, have speedily been put beyond the reach of further offence.

Sometimes the punishment wasn't as severe as this story from NSHS reports of 1893 indicates:

Nebraska City, like other frontier towns, had some hard cases to deal with, and when the courts seemed lax, or slow, the people were ready to lend a helping hand. In the winter of 1860–61, a couple of worthless fellows were strongly suspected of being horse thieves, and with "I guess so" evidence, an angry mob gathered and determined to tie the fellows to a post in the street, and give each one about forty lashes on the bare back. The mob was lead [sic] by Nick Labow (rather a tough character himself). The inferior one of the two was led out, stripped and tied, underwent the terrible ordeal and meekly received the warning to take his departure immediately. The second fellow was much the great rascal, without doubt, but he was smart, and plucky to the last. He defied the mob and hurled anathemas and maranathas at them without stint. Finally he awakened the sympathy of Isaac Core, a prominent citizen of the city. He undertook to talk to the mob, and they hooted at him. But Core was made of stern stuff and would not down, and he fairly brow-beat that unruly mob out of countenance. They finally untied the man and sneaked off like whipped curs.

History has all but forgotten the largest and most regimented protective organization: the Anti-Horse Thief Association (AHTA). The AHTA was founded in 1854 by Major David McKee. McKee, of Scot-Irish ancestry, was born in Sangamon County, Illinois, on December 14, 1823. David was the youngest of eleven children born to Thomas (from Kentucky) and Hanna (from Pennsylvania) McKee. He received his education in a log schoolhouse in Schuyler County, Illinois, and lived at home until he was about eighteen. McKee married seventeen-year-old Martha J. Keesecker in 1842. Six years later the family moved to Clark County, Missouri, after a brief stay in Farmington, Iowa.

Curiously, the farmer and blacksmith raised three elk and broke them to work the farm. He corresponded with the great showman P. T. Barnum, who offered McKee a good sum of money to take two of them to New York and drive their carriage down Broadway. McKee sold half interest in the elk to John D. Smith before they started for New York. During the trip, the two men caught quite a bit of attention from people who stared in disbelief at the elk pulling their carriage. During the ten days the men spent in New York, they were always in the company of newspaper reporters, and children would follow them down the sidewalks as the elk moved through the streets. Before leaving, they sold the elk, and McKee commented, "I always thought I got well paid for my elk speculation, I got $56.00 in money and $1,000 worth of experience and fun."

He got caught up in the excitement of the California gold rush and headed west with three other men. While McKee worked the gold fields, lawlessness was rampant. There were no written laws, no peace officers, and no courts. McKee banded together with other men who desired peace and safety, and formed a code of morals that they enforced. Violators were quickly arrested, given a fair trial and a suitable penalty. From this decision there was no appeal, no delays, no paroles, and no pardons. "They brought order out of chaos," W. W. Graves, editor of the AHTA *Weekly News*, later wrote.

In 1853, McKee returned from California and found that Clark County was a hotbed of criminal activity. Here there *were* laws, but there were many more outlaws than the local officers could handle. The next year, he held an organizational meeting of the AHTA in a schoolhouse near Luray.

McKee's life would be full of success and sorrow. On November 25, 1855, his wife Martha died, after seven children were born to the family. The following year he married Elvira Breeding.

Before the AHTA had a strong footing, the Civil War broke out, and most of the members, including McKee, joined the Union army. In June 1861, he became a private of the 1st Regiment, Northeast Missouri Home Guard. He was later commissioned a major of a cavalry unit that had been merged into the 7th Missouri Cavalry. He fought in engagements all over Missouri until receiving an injury that resulted in his discharge, in 1863. After returning home, he held more meetings and reorganized the AHTA. The first annual meeting of the Grand Order was held October 3, 1864, at Memphis, Missouri, near where the infamous stock detective Tom Horn had been born four years earlier.

Smaller lodges started forming in Missouri as well as Iowa. When the Missouri members chased a thief into Iowa, the two groups worked together. The Iowa group would find out where the Missouri "Antis" were crossing the border on their way home and would meet them at the border with the prisoner. This is how they completed the requisition (extradition) of prisoners who crossed the state line.

By 1865, membership was 4,973, which included 184 suborders. This phenomenal growth continued into the early twentieth century. Major McKee took a firsthand approach to catching thieves in the area and was famous for his successful use of disguises, which even fooled his children on one occasion. He was obviously a man who wasn't popular with criminals, to the extent that an attempt on his life was made at his home while the family was having supper. McKee had bolted the strong door of his house, which prevented the outlaws from knocking it down with a battering ram. Open death threats also greeted him periodically.

McKee traveled to the 1893 Chicago World's Fair and his notes include many observations such as this one: "The Pennsylvania display is good, it has the old bell that tolled our Independence; and the chair Lord Cornwallis used daily at his headquarters in Yorktown in 1781, when it was surrendered to American troops, I sat in Cornwallis' chair while writing the above."

After a long illness with face cancer, Major David McKee, age seventy-two, died on March 7, 1896, at his home in Kahoka, Missouri. Between his two wives, they had nineteen children. McKee was laid to rest in the Kahoka cemetery according to the rights of the Masonic Order. The original gravestone was replaced in 1937 by a monument made of red syenite granite. Members of the Anti-Theft Association (ATA), as it was then named, and residents of Clark County purchased the new monument for $650. It is eight feet long, almost four and a half

feet high, and weighs approximately five tons. His wife Elvira died in
1910 and is buried at the same place. In addition to the couple's names,
the legend on the monument reads, "Major David McKee Founder of
the Anti-Horse Thief Association near Luray, Missouri Erected by the
Anti-Thief Association."

A description of the AHTA would include both detection and
protection. Whenever property was stolen from a member, the group
worked to recover the property and capture the thief; it was fraternal,
semisecret, and patriotic order; no illegal activity was allowed, but a
certain amount of secret work being necessary to accomplish its aim.
It permitted only law-abiding men to belong; no drunkards, debt-
dodgers, or loose-mouthed people were eligible, and it strove to uphold
the law of the land. Those eligible for membership had to be an honest
citizen over twenty-one years of age. Women could join and be under
the protection of the association but could not attend regular meetings
of the order.

Grave monument of Major David McKee, founder of the Anti-Horse Thief Association, at Kahoka, Missouri. The marker is 8 feet long, 4½ feet high and weighs
nearly five tons. COURTESY CHAD PENN

New-member initiations were sometimes exciting. During one such meeting, a fight broke out between two members who were immediately ordered out of the hall. A few minutes later, the doorkeeper rushed in and said the two had armed themselves and were coming back in. The two combatants, still arguing, reentered and commenced to shoot at each other. The terrified new-member initiate joined the others in finding cover under the tables. The guns, as it turned out, were loaded with blanks. Thus completed the first phase of the initiation.

The motto of the AHTA was "Protect the innocent, bring the guilty to justice," with the doctrine, "Let no guilty man escape" and "Thou shall not steal." "Let no guilty man escape if it can be avoided" was used in an 1875 letter by President Ulysses S. Grant, in reference to exposure of the Whiskey Ring, which was a secret association of distillers and federal officials who were defrauding the government.

The lodges continued to spread, which generated the need for uniform activities. The Grand Lodge was organized at Millport, Missouri, in October 1863. Major McKee was chosen for the G. W. (Grand Worthy) president, G. W. vice-president was William Beach, G. W. secretary was William Earhart, and G. W. treasurer was William Grant, along with members G. W. Marshall and Henry McKee.

During the war, the border states seemed to attract a great number of criminals, who were almost free to roam unmolested by the demoralized court systems. The effective work done by the AHTA attracted decent men to their ranks and new lodges multiplied. E. Hitt Stewart, who served two terms as president of the Missouri Division, compared the association's effectiveness with the premiere detective organization of the day when he said, "It isn't every man that Pinkerton gets after that he catches. The AHTA, in a years [sic] time scores as good a per cent at catching criminals as does Pinkerton. There is a vast difference, however, between them, Pinkerton will work on a case if there is enough money in it . . . the Anti-Horse Thief Association will work hard to convict a man for stealing an old hen as though he had stolen a hundred dollars." It was also said that "All farmers cannot get to be Pinkerton detectives, but all good honest men, farmers, judges, mechanics, lawyers, ministers and men of any station, who are found worthy, can get to be Antis and assist in putting down crime which has grown to such alarming extent in the United States."

The central lodge was subdivided into state divisions in 1881. The first constitution of subordinate orders read in part, "This society shall consist of a president, vice-president, secretary, treasurer, marshal and *vigilance committee*." The purpose of the "vigilance committee" was to receive persons arrested by the Antis and investigate the case to determine if there was sufficient cause to turn the prisoner over to officers of the law for prosecution. Because of the negative connotation that "vigilance committee" had earned, the name was changed to "investigating committee." They were still explaining this in 1897, as indicated in a statement by G. N. Sansom for the *Keokuk Gate City*: "In the first place they are styled vigilantes, this is not the old vigilance committee."

B. P. Hanan organized the first suborder of the AHTA in Kansas, on August 5, 1876, in McPherson County. By 1909, there were twenty thousand registered members in Kansas.

A common misconception at the time was that the association only pursued horse thieves. While the AHTA was organized originally for the purpose of conserving property rights in horseflesh, its usefulness was greatly extended. All thefts and violation of criminal laws came within the scope of the orders. Members declared, "A little thief will grow into a big one if left unmolested, hence we treat them all alike and go after the little thief as quickly as the big one." A lodge would, for example, spend $10 to recover a $1 whip. It wasn't the value of the item stolen but the lesson it taught.

The goal of the AHTA was explained this way: "The order seeks to convince thieves that it is extremely hazardous to steal from a member of the order, likewise that they cannot profit by it." Members posted signs on their property that read, "This farm is protected by the A.H.T.A." It was said that some crooks would pass by the home of an Anti and steal a horse of a lower value from a neighbor who hadn't joined the order. The thieves reasoned that it would be easier to run from one man than many. The criminal element was aware of the horseshoe lapel pin, with the horse and rider in the center, and learned to be wary of those wearing it. The pin was the official emblem of the AHTA. The meaning of the horseshoe, in part, as cited by the AHTA, was, "It stands for humanity, charity, and justice . . . it reminds us of our rule of conduct: Do unto others as ye would that others should do unto you . . . it reminds us that service to one's own community is the mark of good citizenship and the foundation of good government . . . as an emblem it inspires us to strive at all times and on all occasions to live up to the ideals of the Order."

The AHTA asserted that it was in no way a lawless "vigilante" group. They answered queries by explaining that they were a law-abiding organization and would not violate one law to vindicate another. Members stated that they opposed mob violence and were a thief-catching association that did not pass judgment on its captives but turned them over to law officers, who saw that they were processed as the law provided.

Even though the organization asserted that they were not a "vigilante" group, occasionally, rumors surfaced that "the Antis had been out," when a man was found early in the morning hanging from a tree. According to Oklahoma history, an AHTA group from Craig County tracked down a young Cherokee who was found with a stolen horse. He was hanged after he denied stealing the animal. The Anti-Thief Association (ATA—name changed in 1926) made an interesting statement on the subject in 1934: "Contrary to the opinion held by some, the Anti-Horse Thief Association *seldom, if ever* [author's italics], swung a captive from the limb of a tree."

On the other side of the coin, however, the danger involved in chasing criminals was illustrated in another case from Craig County, Indian Territory (now Oklahoma). In October 1900, J. I. Poole of Welch, a member of the pursuing committee, was killed while attempting to catch an Arkansas horse thief.

The AHTA believed that it prevented crime and was a public benefactor, "for a thief in jail can steal of no man." The association made the claim, "The AHTA has come nearer to solving the problem of dealing with thieves and criminals than all the officers and philosophers combined." It held the principle that all men were endowed with the inalienable rights of life, liberty, and peaceable possession of their property.

The preamble of the AHTA National Constitution read: "We, the citizens of several states, comprising the National Order of the Anti-Horse Thief Association, for the protection of ourselves against the depredations of thieves, robbers, counterfeiters, incendiaries, vagrants and all other criminals, do hereby pledge ourselves to cooperate with the civil authorities in bringing to justice all such offenders, aiding each other in the recovery of stolen property, do mutually agree to be governed by the following Constitution."

The AHTA was composed of three types of orders: the national order, state orders or divisions, and suborders or lodges. The national was made up of officers and delegates from state orders. The state order was officers and delegates from the suborders within its jurisdiction. The suborders were made up of individual membership. All subordinate orders were required to reelect a new board and investigating committee annually. A pursuing committee was to be appointed by the president every twelve months. The pursuing committee was comprised of two parts. Committee No. 1, which consisted of two or more members and upon the directive of the president, hunted in pairs for suspects. Committee No. 2 was made up of the member whose property was stolen and two others, who would be assigned to pursue the thief. Upon capture, the members would deliver the accused to the investigating committee, who would examine the case. If sufficient evidence existed, they would deliver the thief to civil authorities.

The association divided up the state divisions and laid out their jurisdictions as follows:

Missouri Division—Over Missouri, Iowa, Arkansas, and Louisiana
Illinois Division—Over Illinois, Michigan, Indiana, and all territory south of the Ohio and east of the Mississippi rivers, not otherwise districted.
Oklahoma Division—Over Oklahoma
Indian Territory Division—Over Indian Territory and Texas
Kansas Division—Over Kansas, Nebraska, and all territory north, west, and south not otherwise directed.
Ohio Division—Over Ohio

Each subordinate order kept a "black book," like those used by some cattlemen's associations, that included the names and addresses of all suspicious characters, known criminals, and rejected candidates. Some of the entries in the 1901 Oklahoma black book are amusing:

Dr. Stansbury, perjurer and all around fraud. A thief sympathizer, a regular family disturber.

Bill Crosland, aged 22, sandy complexion, no moustache, height 5 ft 8 inches, heavy build, about 170, blue eyes. Occupation farming; hog, cow and horse thief. Convicted of murder at Danville, Ark. Jan. 1900.

Joseph Dewitt, an old soldier; weight 200 pounds. Light complexion, has a peculiar squint to one eye. Skipped his bills.

E.F. Cochran, deputy U.S. marshal, for shielding and protecting criminals. [Could this have been due to the deputy not turning over a prisoner for lynching?]

Jim Williams, aged about 30, height 5 ft. 11 inches, light hair, weight 150, slightly deaf, has been shot through the temples. Residence with Ben Hughes, 4 miles southeast of Cloud Chief. Horse thief.

Mint John, height 5 ft 9 in., weight 150, light complexion, sandy moustache, 30 years old—noted for pure cussedness of all kinds.

Wm. Happerset, about 22 years old, full smooth face, small light eyes, wears hat well over eyes; back part of head quite prominent; somewhat bowlegged; wt. about 160. Wanted by No. 24, Lahoma [indicates AHTA Lodge No. 24, at Lahoma].

John W. Wall was credited with originating the idea of chartering a special train to chase thieves more efficiently. The first success of this technique for the Antis was used when a Parsons, Kansas, policeman helped others rob a local store of thousands of dollars' worth of furs. Policeman Weggen was sent to prison. The local sheriff or town marshal couldn't afford the cost of using the train, but the price was cheap for the 400 Antis who shared the cost. Wall became known as a born detective due to his score of arrests.

The *Topeka Capital* reported an activity of the association: "Hundreds of miles of telephone lines have been built by members of the A.H.T.A. for the double purpose of keeping in touch with each other and general betterment of the country." The phone system paid off with the capture, in 1907, of Bill Rudolph near Paola, Kansas. Rudolph had robbed the bank in Ironton, Missouri, killing a Pinkerton detective in the process. Rudolph was pursued and taken into custody in Boston, Missouri. He was lodged in the St. Louis jail, where he escaped during a riot he initiated. His next stop, unfortunately for him, was Louisburg, Kansas, where he robbed the depot and left with a team. As he tried to flee the area, he was surrounded by "farmers" carrying shotguns, Winchesters, and revolvers. Rudolph was returned to Missouri, where he was convicted of murder and hanged. The newspaper had reported that a "gang of farmers" made the capture, but every farmer in that gang was there in response to the call made to him by their lodge president, over that rural telephone.

The National Constitution also provided that any division had the privilege of selecting its own name, provided it remained subject to the laws and regulations of the National Order. AHTA divisions with various names met at the Antis convention in Topeka, Kansas, on October 2, 1879. Some of those represented were:

Tornado Vigilance Committee, Ridgeway, Ks.
Citizens' Protective Association of Tecumseh, Shawnee Co., Ks.
Farmers Protective Association of Clay County, Clay Center, Ks.
Langdon Lodge No. 43, Anti-Horse Thief Association, Reno Co., Ks.
Harvey County Horse Protective Association, Newton, Ks.
Mission Creek Vigilance Committee, Wabaunsee Co., Ks.
Glenwood League, Leavenworth Co., Ks.
Wabaunsee County Detective Police, Alma, Ks.

During this AHTA convention, the Kansas State Stock Protective Association was created. The association was designed to allow members of several organizations to work together against stock thieves for the protection of livestock and for their own mutual benefit and protection. They were to influence county commissioners of each county to post a standing reward of $200 for the arrest and conviction of anyone stealing stock. In addition, they asked the various organizations to issue two membership certificates to members to prominently post in the living room of their home and in their stable. These were the only two activities outlined in that first meeting.

In 1901, W. W. Graves began publication of the *A.H.T.A. Weekly News* in St. Paul, Kansas. The paper was officially adopted by the national order in February 1902. The *News* was usually four pages long and cost fifty cents per week. It listed notices and descriptions of property lost or stolen from members and descriptions of men wanted for crimes. The officers of each suborder were required to subscribe to the *News*, which was paid for by the general fund of the order. Graves was a member of AHTA Lodge No. 29 of St. Paul.

In 1902, another AHTA newspaper, *The Searchlight*, began publication in Guthrie, Oklahoma (Indian Territory). James Kirkwood was the editor and publisher of the paper, which came out twice a week.

Members of the AHTA were mostly farmers, but the organization welcomed people from all walks of life, including lawmen, ministers, educators, and congressmen. Membership was listed along with other notable fraternal organizations in biographical sketches of the time. Here is an excerpt of one such bio from Cutler's *History of the State of Kansas*: "E.D. Bugbee, farmer, Republic County, was born in Ashtabula County, Ohio, in 1843 . . . emigrated to Kansas in 1871, located to Republic County. . . . He is a member of John Brown Post No. 44, G.A.R., Belleville Lodge No. 127, A.F. & A.M., and of the Anti-Horse Thief Association."

An incentive was offered for enlisting new members. The *AHTA Weekly News* of March 13, 1902, included a letter from Kansas state president C. G. Horn:

WORK FOR THE GOLD BADGE
Everything in the AHTA is in fine shape as far as I know. We have about 47 new Orders since the state meeting and a number more

in sight. Now a word to deputies: Remember the gold badge. Get to work and organize three or more Orders and get that gold badge as a premium when we meet at Paola next fall.

The "badge" is presumed to be the horseshoe pin, the official emblem of the AHTA mentioned earlier. In reference to a badge, it was stated, "The members of the association have a simple badge—a horse shoe button, which they wear with no spirit of ostentation." In the same edition of the *News*, a description of the Oklahoma badge is given: "The official badge of the Oklahoma jurisdiction is of uniform coin silver, shape of a horse shoe, with horses [*sic*] head protruding, four nails, and the letters A.H.T.A." An advertisement also appeared that offered an AHTA button for ten cents, described "made of celluloid, handsomely lithographed in colors, with design of horse shoe and horse and rider, with letters, A.H.T.A on the horse shoe."

Every issue of the *News* included letters and reports solicited by the editor from members. These letters provide insight into the activities of the Antis, which for the most part were lawful and effective. For those who condemned the association as just another vigilante group, a letter that appeared in the March 6, 1902, issue did little to dissuade their beliefs. The letter from L. T. Marshall, No. 22, McCune, Kansas, reported that members of the lodge went after two chicken thieves and surrounded the field they were hiding in. When they tried to run, one was killed by shotgun blasts, and the other made it to a corn crib, where the thief crawled underneath. The Antis demanded the thief surrender, which he refused to do, so they shot him and dragged him out. The letter concluded with "They proved to be the notorious chicken thieves Mr. and Mrs. C.O. Yote."

Horse thieves of all types continued their vocation, as indicated by several articles about an unusual group. A horse and buggy was stolen from Fort Scott, but the thief was arrested in Baxter Springs, fifty-eight miles away. The thief was described, "The woman is an attractive blonde, about 23 years of age, and calls herself Birdie McCarty. She is believed to be a member of an organized band now working in this section." About two weeks later another report on her ran, which said that McCarty, Cora

Williams, and Hattie Marshall, who were charged with grand larceny, escaped from the Fort Scott jail. They were recaptured after a few hours, plus three men were arrested for helping them escape. The Birdie McCarty saga ended two months later when the *News* reported that Birdie was sentenced to five years in prison, but Judge Simons offered to reduce the sentence by one year if she could recite the Lord's Prayer. He had asked her sometime before court, and she had told him she could recite the prayer. He asked her again in court, reminded her that it would take a year off the sentence, but she admitted that she couldn't recite it. She went to prison for five years.

Notices of strayed or stolen animals and property also appeared in the *News*. Some were amusing: "One bay horse, has had shoulders sore but are well now and has not haired out yet, carries a low head, has big flat feet, right hind foot white, a little hog backed, weighs about 1100 pounds, blind in one eye, foretop clipped off but rather long, G.W. Patchett, No. 197, AHTA."

Many articles dealt with the controversy of where AHTA members could brand their animals and what brand should be used. Lodge No. 17, Parsons, Kansas, decided to use the figure "7" and branded the right front hoof, on the outside below the hair line. They also branded harnesses, saddles, wagons, and meat. They were of the opinion that each lodge should register their own brand with the association's state secretary. Lodge No. 589, Owasso, Indian Territory (I.T.), didn't think branding on the hoof was a good idea as it couldn't be seen without close inspection. They reported that they had tried this method previously and it was a failure. Lodge No. 304, Turle, I.T., used a brand in the shape of a horseshoe, toe up, on the left shoulder of horses.

The May 29, 1902, issue featured one of many success stories of the AHTA. Ned Jackson, alias Frank Pierce, came from Illinois to Kansas, stealing a mare at St. Paul and riding to Erie, where he stole a saddle. Antis at Lodge No. 29 at St. Paul were called out to hunt for the horse and thief. They located both at a livery in Cherryvale, where the thief was attempting to sell the horse. He was taken back to St. Paul and lodged in jail.

The lodge at Owasso, I.T., wrote a letter requesting clarification of a very relevant subject. The *News* published the letter: "By the request of our lodge I write to you to learn if we have the power to search for stolen goods and arrest a person and hold until an officer can be got. In this country of long distances it might not be advisable to wait for an officer to make the first arrest. Please publish your answer on the *News* so all can get the benefit. W.E. Mendell."

The editor replied that, not being familiar with territorial laws, he couldn't give a satisfactory answer. He did explain, "In Kansas the Antis by strategy or otherwise sometimes search premises but they are usually pretty sure the property is there before hand. They also take charge of criminals before getting a warrant if there is danger of the fellow escaping before the warrant may be obtained, but they hold him only long enough to get the necessary papers." The reply went on to say that if the stolen property were found, the man arrested and convicted, there would be no problem. If the property is not found and the suspect is not convicted, he may bring action for personal damages against those who searched and arrested him without authority. "However, very few such actions are ever brought and many of them fail to do the fellow bringing the action any good," the editor added. He recommended that the best procedure would be to guard the premises while the necessary papers were being obtained and hold the suspect if he tried to escape, until papers arrived. It was pointed out that all this would be unnecessary if the suspected thief gave his permission to search the premises.

The pride of being a member of the Anti-Horse Thief Association is shown in a letter published in the *Weekly News* from Lodge No. 293, at Afton, I.T. Some horses and cattle had been stolen near town and deputy US marshals asked for the AHTA's assistance in arresting the thieves. Fifteen members of the lodge helped arrest S. Kelley and Hi Landrum, who were deposited in the Vinita jail. Member T. A. Jackson submitted a letter to the paper, which said in part, "If a fellow wants to be arrested and be arrested quick, just steal from an Anti and he will get his dose quick, but these fellows did not steal from an Anti, but we just wanted to show the US marshals what we could do and we did just what we aimed to when we started."

The AHTA absorbed several local organizations through the years. One of those was the Osage Antithief Society, which was formed in

1884, in Miami County, Kansas. It brought sixty-five new members to the AHTA in 1901.

An article titled "Lynching-Law Facts" appeared in the *News* that was quite enlightening. It reported that the *Chicago Tribune* had been keeping a record of lynchings in the United States since 1885. Since the recording began, the only states that hadn't experienced a lynching were Massachusetts, New Hampshire, Rhode Island, and Utah. It said, "Mob law is thus shown to be the distinct manifestation of no section. The far west has dealt out a great deal of it to horse and cattle thieves." Out of 2,516 lynchings recorded from 1885 to 1900, 2,080 were in the southern states, the highest numbers in Mississippi, Texas, Louisiana, Georgia, Alabama, and Tennessee. Of these victims, 1,678 were Negroes, 801 whites, 21 Indian, 9 Chinese, and 7 Mexicans. These killings were attributed to 114 different offenses, with murder and criminal assault heading the list. "One man was lynched for slapping a child, another for kilting a girl, two paid the penalty for writing insulting letters, two for gambling, three for being unpopular and two for practicing voodooism." The paper went on to explain that as late as 1901, there were 135 lynchings and only 118 legal executions. During the recorded period, it stated that more than fifty women had been victims of lynchings. Indiana led the northern states with thirty-six "mob murders" (possibly due to their Horse Thief Associations law). For comparison, the paper reported there were 90 lynchings in 1881, with 135 in 1901. During this period, 1892 was the highest, with 235 lynchings.

Various publications were produced by the AHTA to help make the organization uniform and knowledgeable and for publicity purposes to attract new members. In July 1903, the Kansas AHTA published a twelve-page pamphlet of information titled "The Anti-Horse Thief Association and How to Organize a Sub-Order." Members were asked to carry them in their pockets and offer them to persons inquiring about the AHTA. In 1905, *Weekly News* editor W. W. Graves ran an advertisement for his new book, "Tricks of Rascals," at twenty-five cents for paper, or fifty cents for a cloth cover. The book was 122 pages long, "full of interesting reading and things all members of the AHTA and CPA [Central Protective Association] should know." Topics included the spotter, barn

The

Anti-Horse Thief Association

Proceedings of the Twenty-Fifth Annual

Session of the

West Oklahoma Division

Held at Enid, Oklahoma

1919

Anti-Horse Thief Association booklet for the 25th annual session of the western Oklahoma division at Enid, 1919. AUTHOR'S PHOTO burners' cheap traveling, borrowed names, the registered horse fake, fences, cattle thieves, backwoods rendezvous, horse whisperers, tricks of bootleggers, the lightning rod man, bogus officers, and schools of crime.

In 1910 the Kansas Bankers Association became an AHTA member. Bank commissioner J. N. Dolley wrote a letter to AHTA president Wall commending the work of the association and stated that he was confident that being a member would result in "materially stopping the wholesale robbery of banks in Kansas."

The AHTA would claim in the neighborhood of fifty thousand members just prior to the start of World War I, which would prove to be the zenith of popularity for the association. During the period 1917–1918, the attention of members was shifted to the war. At a time when the AHTA seemed to be regaining a footing, a depressed economy in the early 1920s affected growth. Not long afterwards, the Ku Klux Klan (KKK) jumped into the national limelight, reviving itself with attacks against blacks all over the South and Midwest. The KKK originated in

1866 for the purpose of terrorizing blacks to keep them from voting. The original group was disbanded in 1869 but was reorganized again in 1915. For various reasons, many AHTA members joined the Klan.

By the 1920s, the popularity of the automobile had swept over the country, pushing construction of new roads and highways from coast to coast. Autos provided much faster transportation and started to replace the horse as *the* item to steal. At an AHTA meeting in Manhattan, Kansas, on October 21, 1915, members agreed to include automobiles within the protection of the organization. From then on, members who

A rare Anti-Horse Thief Association badge of Kansas member Floyd McElroy.
AUTHOR'S PHOTO

owned autos would place a distinctive mark on them, which was registered with the state secretary. That made it easier to spot and recover
stolen autos. Two years later, the Kansas AHTA established a model law
that required filing a registration with the secretary of state whenever
an auto was sold or traded, and to provide for a penalty for those with
mutilated engine numbers.

The fifty-fourth annual session of the National Order of the Anti-
Horse Thief Association was held in Las Vegas, New Mexico, in 1916.
The statistics offered in the official proceedings illustrated the effective-
ness of the group. Here are some that compared the Kansas Division
(Kansas, Nebraska, and all territory north, west, and south) with the
Indian Territory Division (Indian Territory and Texas):

	KANSAS DIV.	*I.T. DIV.*
No. of horses stolen	27	7
No. of horses recovered	24	12(?)
Value of horses recovered	$2650	$375
No. of mules stolen	2	1
No. of mules recovered	2	1
Value of mules recovered	$500	$150
No. of cattle stolen	10	21
No. of cattle recovered	6	7
Value of recovered cattle	$510	$125
No. of saddles stolen	7	14
No. of saddles recovered	5	8
Value of recovered saddles	$95	$184
No. of autos stolen	20	N/A
No. of autos recovered	16	N/A
Value of autos recovered	$7640	N/A
No. of thieves caught	66	53
No. of thieves convicted	59	27
No. of new members initiated	1792	N/A
Largest lodge, Coffeyville, no. members	800	N/A
No. of lodges with 100 or more members	28	N/A

The stats for the Kansas Division also included a number of lodges in Colorado but listed only one in Nebraska, which was No. 467, Litchfield (Theodore H. McCosh, president, and Arther Minshull, secretary). A lodge had been formed in Adams County, Nebraska, in 1895 with 210 members but was disbanded in 1926. Hall, Madison, Otoe, and other lodges did exist in Nebraska as well.

By 1918, the association was trying to recruit new members and had something to brag about. Over the prior year, forty-six member-owned automobiles were stolen, with forty of these recovered by the association. The cost of recovering that stolen property was included in the modest fees of $1 to join and $1 per year membership dues.

The "horse" was officially dropped from the organization's name in 1926 because the low prices of horses made them less valuable to steal, at a time when the popularity of the automobile was skyrocketing. The Anti-Thief Association (ATA), as it became known, continued on for many years, making a partial transformation from a crime-fighting organization to a social one. The September 9, 1969, edition of the *Wichita Eagle* reported on the ATA convention held in Caldwell, Kansas: "Sunday marked the opening of the 107th annual convention of the national order of the Anti-Thief Association. Members also opened the 88th annual state convention." An ATA member explained that they were still active in watching for crime and un-American activities. When a member reported a possible crime, the investigating committee (members who were deputized by local sheriffs) would gather as much evidence as possible and turn it over to law officers.

In addition to groups listed earlier, the state of Oregon also had AHTA lodges. One of these was called "The Oregon Rangers" and had been formed in 1889. The Clarion County (Pennsylvania) AHTA was formed in 1868, and over one hundred years later still held an annual dinner. Now purely a social organization, it is called the "Leatherwood Anti-Horse Thief Association."

The AHTA was sometimes confused with an organization in Indiana called the "Horse Thief Detective Association" (HTDA), originating in 1844. The "Horse Thief Associations Law," passed by the Indiana legislature in 1852, authorized the formation of companies for "the "detection and apprehension of horse thieves and other felons." Under this law, citizens were allowed to organize, given the arrest powers of constables, and allowed legal capability to recover stolen property. Governor Ashbel P. Willard reported in 1859 that many associations had been established under the law, and "regrettably, many individuals were arrested and punished without benefit of lawful trials."

In the 1920s, the HTDA became a part of the Ku Klux Klan for the purpose of prohibition enforcement. The overzealous enforcement activities included the indiscriminate (and extralegal) stopping and searching of cars and persons. From 1922 to 1923, over three thousand prohibition arrests had been made, but the manner in which the HTDA operated caused many travel associations to ban travel to Indiana!

CHAPTER 7

Modern Brand Inspectors and Agencies

AFTER MORE THAN 130 YEARS OF COMBATING RUSTLERS WITH ARRESTS, lynchings, livestock inspection, branding, and recording laws, the livestock thief is still alive and well. These crimes may not be as frequent as they were in the Old West, but theft and other related offenses are still prevalent enough today to justify the need for a specialized law enforcement agency in each of the seventeen western states.

In the West, livestock still roam large pastures and some open government ranges, which makes them just as hard for ranchers to keep an eye on as it was long ago. Although it's helpful if the modern rustler has some working knowledge in handling animals, that is not always the case. The methods and types of transportation have changed with the times, with anything from GPS-equipped tractor-trailer rigs to compact hatchback automobiles having been used to steal livestock. Some thieves butcher cattle right on the spot using chainsaws, while some have had semitrucks outfitted with processing equipment so they can butcher the cattle as they drive down the highway. Vehicles make it easy to transport stolen stock over great distances in a relatively short time. In many cases, some time passes before the theft is discovered, which gives the thieves better chances to escape.

Generally, cattle thefts spike during high market times, but inspectors also have to be aware of other types of crimes that have increased in the twentieth century when prices are low. Insurance fraud, reporting the theft of stock that didn't exist, or reporting losses greater than they actually were are investigated by inspectors as well.

In a two-part article by Bob Hewitt, "A Look at Brand Inspection in the West," which appeared in *Western Horseman* magazine, several questions were asked each of the seventeen western states regarding brand books, laws, and regulations. One of the questions was, "Do you have a rustling problem?" All states but one answered yes.

A California rancher learned how effective some rustlers could be. In 1988, he reported the theft of eighty-one Hereford-Angus steers, valued at $53,000. The thieves apparently loaded the cattle onto two trucks and vanished. The third-generation rancher wasn't insured. In only the first half of 1988, over one thousand head of cattle were stolen in California. In Texas during 1987, over four million dollars' worth of stock and equipment were reported stolen.

Signs of the times were illustrated in a US Department of Agriculture report for the year 1995, in which 19,700 animals were stolen, valued at $12.1 million. This figure did not include horses, sheep, and other livestock. Actual figures were undoubtedly higher as ranchers know there is only a small chance that the stock will be recovered, so they often don't report thefts.

The 1990s saw investigative techniques keeping stride with the need due to continual thievery. In 1991, an Illinois farmer discovered that eleven head of cattle he had raised were missing. A man suspected of cattle theft in three states was arrested by Missouri State Highway Patrol investigator Tom Breen at a local sale barn where the thief tried to sell some of the cattle. The Illinois State Police had notified Breen to watch for the suspect, and with Lee Weeks, enforcement supervisor with the Missouri Division of Animal Health, the two men began checking sale barns. The suspect had consigned five head of cattle that were identified by the owner. The case went well, the cattle thief was behind bars, but to get a conviction, the investigation wasn't complete. Without brands, the state had to prove the cattle belonged to the Illinois farmer. Officer Weeks had previously learned at a convention that DNA typing was starting to be used to establish cattle lineage. Blood samples were taken from the stolen cattle, as well as the purported bull and dams from the victim's farm, and sent to a lab in Salt Lake City. At the trial, a specialist from the lab was able to testify that the stolen cattle were the offspring of the stock at the farm. This was the first time a rustler was convicted by DNA evidence in Missouri, a state that loses from $1 to $3 million per year to livestock thieves.

A western Nebraska cattle buyer pleaded guilty in US District Court in Omaha for rigging a bid for the purchase of cattle and mail fraud in 1995. The bid-rigging scheme involved two other men and was investigated by the FBI and Investigator Larry Birth of the Nebraska Brand Committee. The suspect, who was a cattle buyer for a Kansas meat packing company, conspired with two others to submit low bids in the purchase of the cattle from a Minatare, Nebraska, rancher, depriving him of more than $23,000 in profits. After buying the cattle, the suspect resold them to the Kansas company at a higher price, and the three kept the difference. The primary suspect was sentenced by a federal judge to six months of house arrest and ordered him to pay a fine of $20,000, plus $23,367 in restitution.

Investigators for the Nevada Bureau of Livestock Identification assisted other law-enforcement agencies in a case that made national headlines. Thirty-four wild horses had been found shot to death about five miles east of Reno. Three arrests were made in this cowardly, repulsive crime. The suspects were charged with grand theft, grand larceny, and poisoning, maiming, or killing another person's animal.

In 2015, thefts from an Oklahoma rancher resulted in the loss of twelve cows and sixteen calves. The theft represented a loss of about $65,000, which put her operation in financial jeopardy. The teenage thieves were caught.

A new motive for livestock theft has surfaced. Money, of course is the root, but drug use is the reason. Methamphetamines coming in from Mexico remain the drug of choice in rural Oklahoma, as it is in many states. A special ranger for the Texas and Southwestern Cattle Raisers Association, who investigates thefts in Texas and Oklahoma, stated in

TSCRA Special Rangers (left to right), Charles Hodges, Cullen A. Robertson and R. A. "Slim" Hulen, inspecting cattle at a stockyard. TEXAS CATTLE RAISERS MUSEUM

August 2015 that around four thousand head of stock had been reported missing or stolen in the two states up to that date. It is not all due to high market prices, the ranger indicated. He estimated that more than two-thirds of thefts involve drug and alcohol addiction. He reflected on some cases where the stolen livestock were traded directly to a drug dealer for his product.

Once a thief is caught at a Texas auction barn trying to sell stolen cattle, he or she usually heads out of state to a non-brand-inspection state. Inspectors cannot emphasize strongly enough that it is nearly impossible for them to find stolen stock without branding, marking, and state registration and inspection laws in place. When unbranded calves are recovered, it is difficult for the owner to prove they are his.

Inspectors have kept up with technology that helps them do their job. Besides DNA, smartphones now serve as complete handheld brand books and an easy way to check missing and stolen cattle listings. Protection of livestock is a never-ending job.

Arizona Department of Agriculture:
Livestock Inspection

A reporter for the *Arizona Weekly Star* interviewed troubled cattlemen in southern Pima County. The resulting 1882 news article indicated "a fearful state of affairs in that section. Hundreds of cattle have been stolen and sold to butchers in Tombstone, Charleston, Contention, Benson and Tucson." The rustler gang was reportedly made up of Americans and Mexicans. The Americans sold the cattle to butchers and the Mexicans took horses and mules to Sonora, Mexico, to sell. The rustlers were apparently unable to sell the stolen cattle in Sonora because government inspectors there closely checked ownership of cattle. The cattlemen asked for action, and "these stock men give it as their opinion that the plain, simple remedy which should be adopted is the enactment of a law appointing inspectors whose duty it shall be to pass upon all stock killed by butchers, or shipped out of the Territory." The need and desire to appoint authorities to protect livestock interests had begun. The article finished with "The stock industry must be protected and means devised by which these marauders and thieves be checked, or Pima County stock interests will be paralyzed as in other parts of the Territory."

The problem, though, would never completely vanish. In 1919, newspapers reported that the sanitary board had sent its best inspectors and detectives to Cochise County. It was noted that cattle rustling had been reported from other areas of the state as well, just not on the large scale said to exist in Cochise County.

A law passed by the Arizona Territorial legislature on March 10, 1887, created the three-member Territorial Livestock Sanitary Commission and included provisions for the appointment of a territorial veterinary surgeon. On March 19, 1891, the commission appointed the first livestock inspectors who were empowered to enforce livestock laws. The inspectors could be appointed in a particular area when five cattlemen, each of whom owned at least fifty head of stock, filed a petition with the commission.

In 1895, changes in the law transferred the duties of brand recording from the county recorders to the livestock commission. The territory's first brand book was published about two years later. One of the first brands registered with the territory is believed to be the "Crooked H" of Colonel Henry C. Hooker and his Sierra Bonita ranch.

Despite the organization of the sanitary commission, the system of appointed inspectors was apparently not sufficient. In 1898, the *Phoenix Herald* suggested that the best way to rid the territory of cattle thieves was for the legislature to provide a law permitting cattlemen to organize secret "Cattlemen's Detective Associations" in each county. The detectives were to have the power of deputy sheriffs in livestock matters.

When Arizona became a state in 1912, the Territorial Livestock Sanitary Commission became the Arizona Livestock Sanitary Board. Full-time inspectors were paid $150 per month. Part-time inspectors usually held full-time jobs as ranch foremen, cowboys, or local lawmen, and received from $50 to $125 per month, depending on the number of inspections conducted. Reregistering of brands every ten years became a requirement in 1931. After each reregistration, a new brand book was issued. (This law was changed in 1985, reducing the period to five years.)

Although little has been written about livestock law officers, their job can be as hazardous as any other officer. In February 1918, livestock officer Kane Wooten accompanied US marshal Frank Haynes, Graham County sheriff Frank McBride, and Deputy Martin Kempton to the Klondyke area to arrest two brothers for draft evasion and question them about their involvement in cattle thefts. Just before daybreak, the group of lawmen rode up to the cabin where the suspects, John and Tom Power, lived with their father, Jeff. The Powers opened fire on the officers, which left Wooten, McBride, and Kempton lying dead outside the cabin, and Jeff Power dead inside, after the shooting stopped. US marshal Haynes escaped, riding hard to Safford to get help. This incident began one of the largest manhunts ever conducted in Arizona, which spread into New Mexico and south of the border into Mexico. After nearly a month, the two wounded suspects surrendered to US Army troops just south of the border. John and Tom Power were paroled in the 1960s after spending forty-two years in an Arizona prison.

Livestock Inspection is a division of the Arizona Department of Agriculture and employs approximately twenty livestock officers;

Pickup truck of an Arizona Department of Agriculture Livestock Officer. COURTESY ADAM GONZALES

only fourteen of those are full time. The officers are responsible for curtailing livestock theft and assisting the state veterinarian in stopping contagious and infectious stock diseases. Livestock officers are state-certified peace officers and work with an investigative supervisor. Their duties include the enforcement of laws and regulations pertaining to branding, transportation, and sale of cattle, horses, sheep, and other livestock.

General duties of officers and inspectors include the authentication of livestock bills of sale, brands, and marks. They will not grant a certificate of inspection of unbranded hides of stock or those in which the marks and brands cannot be ascertained. An officer has the right to stop any person who is in possession of livestock or hides for the purpose of examining brands, marks, and related shipping or ownership papers, if he has reasonable cause to believe the person has violated state laws relating to livestock. Officers and inspectors can enter any premises where livestock are kept to examine brands and marks, or to determine the health or welfare of the animals.

CALIFORNIA DEPARTMENT OF FOOD AND AGRICULTURE: BUREAU OF LIVESTOCK IDENTIFICATION

A division of the California Department of Food and Agriculture (CDFA) is the Bureau of Livestock Identification. Livestock inspectors within this bureau advise livestock owners on cattle importation requirements, proper sanitary procedures, and eradication of diseases, and supervise the cleaning and disinfecting of areas where stock is kept and the vehicles in which they are transported. The inspectors issue citations and investigate violations of state livestock laws and assist in prosecution of violators. They also help veterinarians in administering animal health inspections and programs. The bureau's inspectors protect stock owners from theft through the regulation of livestock brands and the inspection of cattle prior to sale or slaughter and recording information from these inspections. The inspection program is totally funded through the brand registration and inspection fees. Currently there are 22,145 active brands in California.

Long obsolete California Cattle Protection Special Investigator badge.
AUTHOR'S PHOTO

The California Food and Agriculture Code gives all peace officers in the state the authority to stop any vehicle hauling cattle or horses for the purpose of making an investigation. Every sheriff or police officer who receives a report of loss or theft of any livestock notifies the Bureau of Livestock Identification. The report includes a complete description of each missing animal, including brands and marks, the city or county where the theft occurred, and the approximate date and time of the loss. A bureau investigator is not required to conduct an investigation but usually assists the agency that filed the original report.

Colorado Department of Agriculture: Brand Inspection Division

The Brand Inspection Division of the CDA has a history dating to territorial days. It became a state agency in 1903 and a division of the agriculture department in the 1970s. More than 34,000 livestock brands are currently administered by the division. Brands are used to identify not only cattle and horses but also sheep, mules, burros, elk, and fallow deer.

The governor appoints five members to the State Board of Stock Inspection, who manage the division. The division works with a $2.5 million annual budget that is funded by the inspection fees and brand registration fees that are paid by stockmen every five years. The four primary regulatory duties assigned to the division are recording and administration of livestock brands; inspection of all livestock and verification of ownership before sale; inspecting and licensing of packing plants and sale barns; preventing theft and returning strayed or stolen livestock, and to investigate reports of lost or stolen livestock.

During the 1994–1895 fiscal year, the division inspected over four million head of livestock and identified ownership of lost, stolen, or strayed livestock valued at approximately twenty million dollars. Over sixty thousand horse inspections were conducted and the number of horse travel permits doubled. It is the duty of brand inspectors to inspect the brands and earmarks of cattle, horses, or mules to be transported by train, truck, or other means, within the state or out.

Idaho State Police: State Brand Board

The Idaho Brand Inspector became a division of the Idaho State Police in 2000. Full-time deputy brand inspectors are law-enforcement officers who are required to attain state law-enforcement training certification within a year of hire date. The state brand inspector and his deputies have the powers and duty to enforce all state laws of identification, inspection, and transportation of livestock, along with all laws designed to prevent the theft of livestock. They have the authority and power of peace officers with general jurisdiction throughout the state.

The recording of livestock brands during territorial and early statehood was done by the counties, usually the county clerk. Beginning in

1905, brand recording duties were taken over by various state agencies through the years. The state legislature passed a law that directed the Department of Agriculture to publish a book that listed all registered brands. However, it wasn't until 1936 that the first brand book was issued because the legislature hadn't funded the project.

In 1974, a mandatory brand inspection was enacted, and proof of ownership was required before livestock could be sold. The State Brand Board is funded by inspections, the registry, transferral and renewal of brands, and the sale of brand books.

KANSAS DEPARTMENT OF AGRICULTURE: DIVISION OF ANIMAL HEALTH BRANDS PROGRAM

Looking back at the progression of the agency, in 1939 the state sanitary commissioner became the state brand commissioner (with a brand board), whose duty was to keep all official books and records, and record all brands used for branding or marking livestock. The session laws of 1943 explained another change:

> *Because more and more duties are being given to the State Livestock Sanitary Commissioner (brand commissioner) and these duties concern not only enforcement of sanitary rules and regulations, but also many other and varied responsibilities relating to the promotion of the general welfare of the livestock industry of the state, there is hereby created a commission to be known as the Kansas Livestock Commission which shall consist of seven members, one of which will be the president of the Kansas Livestock Association and six other members appointed by the governor. The State Brand Board is hereby abolished.*

The commissioner appointed the state brand inspectors who, in his judgment, may be necessary to curtail livestock thefts and assist in the enforcement of the provisions of state livestock laws.

The 1974 statute gave brand inspectors authority to arrest persons violating livestock laws. However, by 1995, brand inspectors no longer had arrest powers but continued to assist with investigations.

Today, the Kansas Brands Program is under the Department of Agriculture's Division of Animal Health. The animal health board consists of nine members who are appointed by the governor. The board serves in an advisory capacity to the livestock commissioner and assists him with policy and plan development relating to his office. The Brands Program maintains a registry of over seventeen thousand brands and helps with the market brand inspection program. A special investigator appointed by the commissioner has the authority to make arrests, conduct searches and seizures, and carry firearms while investigating violations of Kansas livestock laws.

MONTANA DEPARTMENT OF LIVESTOCK: BRANDS ENFORCEMENT DIVISION

In 1917 the Montana legislature passed a law that combined the Board of Stock Commissioners and the Board of Sheep Commissioners into the Montana Livestock Commission. The commission was made up of six members who were appointed by the governor, and handled inspection and enforcement for the industry until the reorganization of state government took place in 1969.

The Executive Reorganization Act of 1969 was implemented in 1971, when the livestock commissioner and the Livestock Sanitary Board were combined under the new Department of Livestock. The governor appointed seven members who made up the Board of Livestock. Eighteen district field inspectors and seventeen market inspectors form the enforcement arm of the Department of Livestock.

Inspections include the examination of livestock and all marks and brands to identify ownership. The inspection certificates specify the date of inspection; the place of origin and destination of shipment; the name and address of the owner or applicant for inspection and the buyer; the class of animal; the marks and brands, if any, on the animal; and any other information the department may require.

Livestock criminal investigators are full-time law-enforcement officers and are authorized to stop vehicles carrying livestock; serve search warrants; collect evidence from the field; make arrests; issue citations; seize vehicles, livestock, and other property; and to independently conduct felony investigations. As a sworn peace officer, the inspectors may also be called upon to assist federal, state, and local law-enforcement agencies with arrests, investigations, and road blocks.

NEBRASKA BRAND COMMITTEE

Legislative bill No. 275 was signed by the governor on April 2, 1941, creating the Nebraska Brand Committee (NBC). Secretary of State Frank Marsh was directed to chair the committee and appointed four other members as allowed by the bill. The NBC took over the duties of brand inspection and cattle loss/theft investigation that had been conducted by the Nebraska Stock Growers Association since 1899.

The committee records all brands, brand transfers, and renewals, and publishes a brand book that contains about thirty-five thousand brands. The investigative staff reports thefts or missing livestock and identifies the owners of strays. An average of fifty full-time and sixty part-time brand inspectors cover all cattle moved from any point in the Brand Inspection Area (roughly the western two-thirds of the state) to anywhere outside the area and all cattle that change ownership. Brand inspectors generally carry out the provisions and enforcement of all laws pertaining to brands, brand inspection, and associated livestock laws. Three investigators employed by the committee are commissioned state deputy sheriffs (this gives them statewide jurisdiction) and have the authority to enforce all state statutes pertaining to livestock.

Chase Feagins was the first secretary and chief inspector for the NBC, a position he held until 1958. Before being named chief inspector, Feagins was a cattle buyer for a Denver commission company. His successor was Keith Schneider, a World War II veteran, who held the post for eight years. Arthur C. Thomsen assumed the chief's position in 1966 and retired in 1993. Steven F. Stanec, a South Dakota native, was the fourth chief inspector. An army veteran, Stanec was hired as a brand inspector trainee by the NBC in 1984, before becoming chief ten years later.

Jack Middleton had one of, if not the longest, tenure with the NBC. Starting as a brand inspector, he spent his last sixteen years as an investigator. Middleton's career spanned forty-nine years before he retired in 1986.

Dallas V. Glaze's career spanned over thirty-four years, from 1958 to 1992. He was an inspector until 1972 when he became an investigator. Glaze, like others, carried a trunk full of equipment to do his job. That equipment included binoculars, camera, rope, rifle, powerful spotting scope, hide clippers, portable red light, magnetic door emblems, and an electric branding iron with the "N" brand, which is reserved only for the state. The most significant case Glaze investigated was in the 1970s, when 485 cattle were stolen from a stockman near Wahoo. He tracked the cattle to where they had been sold in Kansas and Missouri.

James C. Mogle, one of the last old-time brand inspectors for the state, started his career with the Nebraska Stock Growers Association in 1936. He was born on the family homestead on the Niobrara River in 1893. Mogle was a cowboy who worked on ranches in northern Nebraska and South Dakota before 1920. He retired in 1966, after thirty years of inspecting brands.

The current executive director of the Nebraska Brand Committee is Bill Bunce, who oversees the four-million-dollar annual budget (totally self-supported through fees) and one hundred employees. Bunce served as executive director of the New Mexico Livestock Board before accepting the same position in Nebraska. Before that he was superintendent of True Ranches, Inc., in Casper, Wyoming, and director of Agri-Business and International Trade for the state of Wyoming.

When asked about the activities of the NBC today, Bunce explained, "These days we see fewer cases involving theft through physical possession of stolen animals, and more frequent theft through misrepresentation, evasion of existing liens, fraud, collusion, racketeering, bad payment, etc. Some of the more heart-wrenching cases involve divorces, family disputes, and contested estates. In cases of interstate crime, the team at GIPSA (US Dept. of Agriculture's Grain Inspection, Packers & Stockyards Administration) are close allies as well." Speaking about branding, Bunce said, "A frustration, like in all law enforcement, is that rock solid cases can take a very long time to successfully prosecute and critical evidence thrown out on technicalities. While some might argue it is medieval, a brand on livestock is still like a coat-of-arms."

NEVADA DEPARTMENT OF AGRICULTURE: LIVESTOCK IDENTIFICATION

Organized livestock law enforcement in Nevada began prior to 1935 when the State Board of Stock Commissioners conducted hide and carcass inspections. In 1935 the Nevada Department of Agriculture, which included the Bureau of Livestock Identification, was authorized by legislature.

The Livestock Identification division consists of seventy-nine deputy brand inspectors, two enforcement officers, an administrator, state veterinarian, program officer, administrative assistant, and laboratory technician. The brand inspectors are paid time and mileage when on duty. The enforcement officers are certified peace officers who investigate reported or suspected cases of livestock theft and assist in the preparation of theft cases for prosecution.

NEW MEXICO LIVESTOCK BOARD

Livestock brands began to be registered with county clerks in 1850, when New Mexico Territory was formed. The Cattle Sanitary Board was established by a bill in 1887 for the purposes of controlling livestock diseases and theft. Included in the bill was a quarantine law because of the diseased cattle entering the area.

On April 6, 1887, the first meeting of the Cattle Sanitary Board convened in Santa Fe. Duties of inspectors were laid out in the new law that said they would inspect brands and earmarks, hides, and slaughter houses, including all cattle transported or driven out of the territory. New laws passed in 1895 added the duties of taking over the brand recording system from the counties, and made branding and recording brands with the board mandatory.

The 1899 Annual Report of the Cattle Sanitary Board of New Mexico lauded their success in fighting rustlers:

> *One very encouraging result of the careful work done by the inspectors of the board, has been to reduce the number of cattle found in herds about to be removed from the territory, for which no legal authority to handle could be shown, from the thousands of a few years ago to less*

than one hundred head during the year last past, and another matter
of utmost importance to the welfare of the whole territory, has been
the vigorous prosecution and speedy punishment of cattle thieves by
the courts, no less than thirty-one of whom have been convicted and
sentenced to penal servitude from the Fourth Judicial District alone
during the year 1899.

One of these inspectors met with a certain amount of fame. Nathan Howard "Jack" Thorp, who was born in New York City, spent his early years working on his brother's ranch in Nebraska. He later moved to New Mexico where he was a cowboy, ranch operator, and state livestock inspector. The fame transpired not from his inspector duties but from his love of the unique music he learned in the West. He collected every song he could find and even wrote some himself. *Songs of the Cowboys* was published in 1908, *Tales of the Chuckwagon* in 1926, and *Pardner of the Wind: Story of the Southwestern Cowboy* in 1941 (posthumously). He also wrote fiction and poetry for various publications and worked for the Works Progress Administration's New Mexico Federal Writers' Project. He was the first person to collect and preserve the early ballads of the West. On June 4, 1940, Thorp died at his Alameda, New Mexico, home.

Rules for the New Mexico inspectors were laid out. They were not allowed to act as an agent of any livestock commission firm or engage in buying or selling of livestock on commission or speculation. They were not allowed to inspect any stock in which they had any ownership interest in, or when they were in the employ of the owner of cattle. The rules explained that "all inspectors will hold their positions at the pleasure of the Board, their time in office being indeterminate . . . regular inspectors will be allowed such actual and necessary expenses as may be agreed upon by the Board and to furnish itemized statements of expenses."

Sheep raising was also popular in the territory, and in 1897, the Sheep Sanitary Board was organized to eliminate diseases and begin a heath inspection program. The two boards existed separately for seventy years, until combining in 1967 to form the New Mexico Livestock Board.

Today, the inspectors for the board are fully certified law-enforcement officers who routinely stop vehicles transporting livestock to check for inspection and ownership papers. As in most western states, New Mexico law states that it is illegal to brand or mark, or deface a brand or mark, that is the property of another. And if a person uses a brand, it must be registered with the state.

NORTH DAKOTA STOCKMEN'S ASSOCIATION

Branding of livestock in North Dakota (the Dakota Territory) began in the 1870s. In those days brand recording was done by various county officials. Due to the inconsistencies of this system, the duties of brand recorder were turned over to the secretary of state in 1890.

The first state-recorded brand was the "two bars" of rancher William Connolly. The earliest brand books were published in 1892 and 1899. The "Little Gem" brand book, sold by George Woodman, contained over 1,300 brands from North and South Dakota, Montana, Wyoming, and Nebraska. These early books seemed to be a popular private enterprise as shown by Van Dersel, who copied brands from state records in 1902 and sold them in book form.

Formed in 1929, the North Dakota Stockmen's Association (NDSA) was incorporated as a nonprofit in 1941. Brand inspection in the state had been conducted by county brand inspectors, veterinarians, and the association until 1949, when the legislature designated the NDSA as the sole entity authorized to conduct brand inspections in the state. The NDSA is a livestock association duly organized under the laws of the state and is registered as a market agency under the Packers and Stockyards Act of 1921 for the better protection of the livestock industry of the state.

The chief brand inspector and two field men employed by the NDSA have the power of a police officer for the purpose of enforcing brand laws and any other state laws or rules relating to livestock. They can make arrests upon view and without a warrant for any violation of North Dakota livestock laws committed in their presence.

OKLAHOMA DEPARTMENT OF AGRICULTURE FOOD AND FORESTRY: INVESTIGATIVE SERVICES UNIT

Although not required by law, livestock brands are applied for and registered with the Oklahoma Cattlemen's Association, which also publishes a brand book every five years. When questions of ownership arise, registered brands do provide prima facie evidence in court. One interesting note regarding brands is cited in section 4-13 of the Oklahoma Brands Laws, which makes the use of the "dog iron" brand used by the late Will Rogers, illegal by anyone other than the State of Oklahoma or a blood relative of Rogers.

Agricultural laws of Oklahoma ranging from livestock theft to wild land arson are enforced by the agriculture department's investigative services unit. Stationed throughout the state are nine investigators who work with local and county police agencies. The investigators are state-certified peace officers.

In addition, Texas and Southwestern Cattle Raisers Association special rangers have police power in Oklahoma under authority of the Oklahoma Bureau of Investigation (OBI). The director of the OBI is authorized to appoint, with commission approval, no more than twenty special officers (TSCRA special rangers) who are not salaried employees of the bureau. They have authority only to enforce statutes relating to livestock or farm and ranch equipment or supplies in Oklahoma.

OREGON DEPARTMENT OF AGRICULTURE: LIVESTOCK IDENTIFICATION DIVISION

The responsibility for recording and inspecting livestock brands belongs to the Oregon Department of Agriculture's Livestock Identification Division. Brands are not required in Oregon, but the state does require inspections of all cattle and horses before being hauled out of state, sold at auction, and before being taken to a slaughter house.

The department appoints employees as brand inspectors to administer and enforce the brand inspection activities. Livestock

Old Oregon Livestock Theft Prevention Service badge. COURTESY STEVE DOWNIE

police officers or investigative officers are employed to enforce related laws and for the supervision of brand inspectors.

Brand inspectors, livestock police officers, and investigative officers are empowered to carry out the activities of peace officers and police officers as set forth in Oregon Revised Statutes chapter 133. They are furnished uniforms, identification badges, emergency vehicles, and other equipment appropriate to carrying out investigative and law-enforcement duties.

SOUTH DAKOTA DEPARTMENT OF AGRICULTURE: STATE BRAND BOARD SOUTH DAKOTA DIVISION OF CRIMINAL INVESTIGATION

The South Dakota legislature established a state brand and mark commission in 1897 that was comprised of the secretary of state and three livestock producers who were appointed by the governor. The commission had the responsibility of brand registration until 1925. In 1899, a brand book was published that contained over two thousand brands.

In 1924, the South Dakota Stock Growers Association was authorized to inspect cattle for ownership at market centers. The Packers and Stockyards Act of 1921 authorized "Any state department, agency, or duly organized livestock association of any state in which branding or marking of livestock prevails by custom or law, to charge and collect a fee for the inspection of brands."

The job of registering brands was transferred to the Department of Agriculture's Division of Animal Industry in 1925. During these years, many conflicting brands were issued due to personnel being unfamiliar with the complicated brand system. To correct the situation, the legislature created the State Brand Board in 1937, a separate state agency. The board originally consisted of three stockmen, nominated by the stock growers' association and appointed by the governor. The legislature assigned supervision of the brand inspection program to the board in 1943. The board contracted with the association for these services. Also in 1943, the legislature created an inspection area that included all counties west of the Missouri River and set a fifteen cents per head fee. Counties on the east side of the river could petition the brand board to be made a part of the inspection area and many did. These counties eventually dropped out, however, with the last one withdrawing in 1980. Surprisingly, statistics at the time indicated that more cattle were east rather than west of the river.

In July 1947, stockmen from Montana, Wyoming, Nebraska, North Dakota, and South Dakota met in Belle Fourche and organized the Five State Livestock Brand Conference. The conference eventually grew to over twenty states and four Canadian provinces, which necessitated a name change to the International Livestock Brand Conference (IBC). The purpose of the conference was to familiarize members with each other, each state's brand laws, and ways of working together to make identification and inspection of livestock more effective. The motto of the IBC is "A cow's only return address is the brand that she carries." There are currently twenty-five thousand registered brands in South Dakota.

On March 1, 1985, the South Dakota Brand Board discontinued use of inspector-investigators (who had police powers) of the stock growers' association and replaced them with brand board employees. Ken Rand was the first full-time livestock investigator for the board. The board employed four investigators for the purpose of enforcing provisions of state livestock laws. They were certified law-enforcement officers who enforce laws statewide pertaining to the inspection, sale, branding, mis-branding, ownership, transportation, or theft of cattle, horses, mules, sheep, and buffalo.

Today the brand board is attached to the Department of Agriculture for reporting purposes only. By 2015, the investigators had been trans-ferred to the South Dakota Division of Criminal Investigation (DCI) under an agreement between the state brand board and DCI.

TEXAS AND SOUTHWESTERN CATTLE RAISERS ASSOCIATION

The first formal body of men who fought cattle thieves for the state of Texas was organized in 1874. Ranger Captain Leander H. McNelly was ordered to form a "special force" of Texas Rangers to stop the rustling along the Mexican border orchestrated by Juan Cortinas. The force wasn't of much help to the ranchers across the state who were also plagued with theft, however. Unfortunately, only three years after taking command of the special force, Captain McNelly died of tuberculosis at age thirty-three.

The Stock Raisers Association of Northern Texas (SRANT), established in 1877, was the foundation of the present Texas and Southwestern Cattle Raisers Association (TSCRA). In 1893 the name was changed to the Cattle Raisers Association of Texas, and it was at this time the livestock inspectors were given authority as "Special Texas Rangers." Texas state law section 411.023 allowed the appointment of special rangers, who are honorably retired commissioned officers of the department, and not more than 300 other persons. Special rangers were subject to orders of the commission and the governor for special duty to the same extent as other law-enforcement officers, except that special rangers could not enforce laws except those designed to protect life and property and could not enforce traffic laws. The inspectors held their "special" commissions until 1919, when the legislature invalidated them. They were renewed in 1924, however, and they have held this authority ever since.

These signs posted by members of the Texas & Southwestern Cattle Raisers Association assure potential thieves that they will be tracked down by Special Texas Rangers of TSCRA. AUTHOR'S PHOTO

The horse still serves TSCRA Special Texas Rangers on occasion, as they do inspectors in many western states. COURTESY TEXAS CATTLE RAISERS MUSEUM

With the SRANT in its early stages, even more effort was put forth in battling stock thieves. In December 1881, the Protective and Detective Association of Texas was chartered in Dallas, with a capital stock of $10,000. Their mission was the protection of stock against thieves, and the detection and conviction of said thieves. The company's livestock was branded with the letter "C." Directors were listed as James H. Duncan, George W. Pfeifer, Jack Duncan, and Kenneth Raynor Jr. A $1000 reward fund was established with plans to hire "experienced detectives."

Inspectors had to exhibit nerves of steel when cowmen disagreed with their claim of stolen cattle. One of the first inspectors for the association, Tom Keeler, was killed by rustlers in 1897 when he found thieves moving stolen cattle across a pasture near Campbellton.

In 1921, the name Texas and Southwestern Cattle Raisers Association (TSCRA) was adopted. The association has over eighteen thousand members in Texas, Oklahoma, and surrounding states. Thirty-three field inspectors are stationed throughout the state. As mentioned in the Oklahoma section, TSCRA has been granted police powers in Oklahoma through the Oklahoma State Bureau of Investigation. The field inspectors supervise eighty brand inspectors who conduct inspections at 140 auction markets. Over six million head of cattle are inspected each year. In 1996, TSCRA inspectors with other agencies, investigated over 1,700 theft cases, and located property valued at $2,312,740.10.

The association publishes a *Missing–Stolen Livestock Bulletin* twice monthly that is sent to a thousand other law enforcement agencies, and they have published the *Cattleman* magazine for over ninety years. Records maintained by TSCRA include over 150,000 brands. Texas has a county-level brand registration system. Farmers and ranchers who own cattle, hogs, sheep, or goats are required to record that person's earmarks and brands with the county clerk in the county in which the animals are located.

Currently, TSCRA special rangers work approximately a thousand agricultural crime cases and recover an average of five million dollars in stolen cattle and assets for ranchers annually.

UTAH DEPARTMENT OF AGRICULTURE AND FOOD: BRAND INSPECTION BUREAU

The Animal Industry Division of the Utah Department of Agriculture and Food is made up of five primary bureaus, one of which is the Brand Inspection Bureau. Brand inspectors are empowered for enforcement of the Utah Livestock Brand and Anti-Theft Act. Their job is to conduct inspections at livestock auctions and all stock prior to changing ownership, leaving the state, or going to slaughter. During 1996, approximately seven hundred thousand cattle and horses were inspected and over one million dollars of stolen/lost livestock were located for their owners.

The Livestock Brand Board was created to work with the agriculture department, directing procedures and policies to be followed in administering and enforcing the brand and theft act. The agency maintains the central Brand and Mark Registry, which includes all brands and marks registered in Utah.

A brand inspector has the authority of a special function officer for the purpose of enforcing brand and theft laws, and the inspectors may, if deemed proper, stop any vehicle carrying livestock or carcasses for the purpose of examining brands, marks, certificates of inspection, and bills of lading or bills of sale. Inspectors may enter any premises where livestock are kept or maintained for the purpose of examining brands and marks. If admittance is refused, the department may immediately obtain an ex parte warrant from the nearest court to allow entry.

WASHINGTON DEPARTMENT OF AGRICULTURE: LIVESTOCK INSPECTION

Registration of livestock brands had been conducted by Washington counties prior to 1935. During that year, the legislature enacted the first laws calling for a state brand registration, but the new law didn't address policing of the livestock laws. This was remedied when the legislature met in 1937, passing a provision that empowered brand inspectors.

Sanford "Sandy" Collins was the first official brand inspector for the state of Washington. He began service to the state in June 1937. Milton Collins, Sandy's father, had moved from Virginia to Colorado, where he established the family ranch in 1887. Sandy was born on November 17,

First Spokane, Washington, brand inspector's office, ca. 1940. Pictured are inspectors Sanford Collins and Grant Hubley. Note brands burned into the building front. COURTESY GEORGE W. COLLINS

1900, at the ranch near Crawford, Colorado. At the age of eleven, he started working as a full-time cowboy. In 1918, he married Delia Davis and built a log house on the ranch. Sandy and Delia relocated to a place near Spokane, Washington, in 1935. New cattle laws passed that year required that cattle sellers provide buyers with a bill of sale, and the cattle had to be branded. Sandy applied for a brand inspector job, but the provision for enforcement hadn't been made yet. He was hired in 1937, though, at a salary of $150 per month. Sandy retired after twenty-eight years of service to the state in 1965. At his retirement, he was presented with a gold badge bearing the number "1."

Sandy's son George was born in 1919. He helped his father inspect while in high school and later served in the 42nd Infantry Division in Europe during World War II. Ten years to the month of Sandy's starting date, George hired on as a state brand inspector in June 1947. He retired in 1993 after forty-six years of full- and part-time work. During that time George was honored by the Walla Walla County Cattlemen's Association as the 1988 Cattleman of the Year, even though he didn't own a single critter. That same year he received the Director's Award from the state agriculture department. The state of Washington dedicated the 1990 edition of the state brand book to George W. Collins.

A Livestock Identification Advisory Board was established to provide advice to the director of the agriculture department. The board assists the director with decisions regarding livestock identification programs, brand inspection, and licensing fees. The director is also the official recorder of brands for the state and publishes the brand book. All officers appointed to enforce laws relating to commission merchants, livestock identification, brand registration, and inspection, and who have completed state criminal justice training, have authority as a peace officer solely for enforcing these laws.

WYOMING LIVESTOCK BOARD

Like many states, brands were first recorded by the counties in Wyoming. The State Board of Livestock Commissioners was created in 1888, which duplicated some of the activities of the Wyoming Stock Growers Association (WSGA). The WSGA was experiencing serious financial difficulties at this time and reluctantly turned over inspection duties to the board in 1890 to cut costs. The association did regain the responsibility for livestock inspection three years later.

The state of Wyoming took over all brand recording in 1909, which was done manually until 1992, when a computer was placed into service. In 1932, acting on a recommendation from WSGA president J. Elmer Brock, the legislature combined the State Board of Livestock Commissioners and the Sheep Sanitary Board and placed the new state agency under the state veterinarian. The new Wyoming Livestock and Sanitary Board worked at protecting livestock from disease and conducted brand inspections. In 1949, the County Brand Inspection Law was enacted, which placed supervision of inspections under the board, but local inspections were done by the sheriff, or undersheriff, with only a few counties employing a full-time inspector.

During the seventy-eighth annual meeting of the WSGA in 1950, held in Cody, Dr. G. H. Good, director of the Livestock and Sanitary Board, gave a report of activities for the fiscal year 1949–1950. The board's inspectors covered ten sales rings in the state, where they inspected 5,182 horses, 27 mules, 31,974 sheep, and 113,436 cattle.

The Brand and Theft Committee of the WSGA reported during the 1960 annual meeting that brand inspection was not effective on the county level and recommended that all brand inspection in the state be placed under the auspices of the Livestock and Sanitary Board, with the WSGA conducting the actual inspections. Again, the powerful association was listened to, as they agreed and made July 1 the start date. A state brand supervisor was appointed and inspectors were assigned a number of districts laid out by the association.

Today, the Wyoming Livestock Board (WLSB) is responsible for the protection of livestock interests in the state from disease and theft. Divisions of the WLSB are law enforcement, animal health, brand inspection, and brand recording.

State brand laws indicate that every stock owner allowing his livestock over six months old to run at large or mingle with livestock other than his own shall brand his livestock with his recorded brand. It is unlawful for anyone to sell and deliver, or remove from any county in Wyoming to any other county, state, or country, any livestock unless each animal has been inspected by a state brand inspector for brands and ownership at the time of delivery. Refusal by the driver of any vehicle to exhibit a certificate of inspection or a properly executed shipper's certificate and agreement, or permit listing the livestock being transported within the state, is justification for any authorized person to hold the vehicle and livestock. If the carrier cannot establish his right to transport the livestock within twelve hours, the vehicle and livestock are impounded.

According to the WLSB 2016 annual report, the operating budget of $17,694,437 represents funding from federal funds, producer-generated revenue from brand recording and inspection activities, and the general fund. The four operational units comprise nineteen full-time staff, including six in administration, seven in animal health, six in brands, and ninety-six at-will brand inspectors. Four WLSB law-enforcement officers are currently on the roster. The report indicated that the agency worked thirteen cases of rustling, seventy-three missing/theft reports, forty-five brand inspection violations, and twenty-three animal health violations. As of February 1, 2017, the WLSB had twenty-five active theft cases that represented 237 head of missing cattle plus 90 head of sheep.

Chapter 8

"They Don't Rustle Cattle Anymore . . . Do They?"

In the early 1930s, *Popular Mechanics* magazine reported, "The fact is, that parts of the west are just as wild as they were in the days of the 'Apache Kid' and 'Wild Bill' Hickok. Men still go armed habitually. Cattle rustlers, 'two-gun' men, and outlaw bands are still active." The title of the article was "Where the West Is Still Wild." This was the era when rustlers really went mobile, with motor vehicles. They would load up a truck and drive to a secluded spot to butcher their haul. Deputy sheriffs and livestock inspectors would follow tire tracks and keep an eye out for circling buzzards.

Popular Mechanics, the fine and long-published magazine that it is, would not be the first periodical one would think of to find articles on cattle rustling. "Trapping Modern Cattle Rustlers" was the title of one such 1939 article in the magazine, so well known for its coverage of modern technology and how-to articles.

Mind you, law-enforcement procedures were a bit different in the late 1930s, but they *were* effective. One rancher reported to stock detectives that he knew he was a victim of thieves due to the constant bawling of some of his cows, which indicated they were missing their calves. With no evidence or leads on the large range, the frustrated detectives decided on who the most logical suspect was. They waited until their "suspect" left on a truck trip and went onto his place and searched. About to give up, one stock detective saw a pair of large shoes. He picked up one, turned it over, and found that a piece of wood carved in the shape of a cow hoof was affixed to the bottom. The thief would park his truck on the road and walk into a range, leaving no tire or shoe prints.

Captain C. E. Mace, of the California Livestock Identification Service, observed that "The rustler had traded in his horse for a fast truck and trailer . . . into which he could speed off at forty miles per hour . . . the next morning unloads at some point several hundred miles away." He explained that a $200 standing reward for cattle rustlers had prompted cowboys to patrol roads and stop any truck hauling cattle to check for proper ownership or shipping papers. He added that gun duels were still fought on the range with officers who had large areas to cover, so they welcomed the help of ranchers.

Mace reported that during 1938, the Livestock Identification Service had arrested over seventy people for stealing cattle, most of those were one or two animals at a time. He explained that the theft problem was north of the border as well and that the Royal Canadian Mounted Police had suggested "nose-printing" cattle (similar to fingerprinting of humans) as an identity check, since it was claimed that all nose-prints of cattle are different. One might think this a silly idea, except for the fact that back in 1922, Dr. W. E. Petersen, a University of Minnesota dairy researcher, extensively reported on the methods of obtaining ink nose-prints, and the use of those prints in identifying dairy cattle. The procedure used in nose-printing cattle is similar to fingerprinting humans but for the use of a headgate to restrain the subject. There is a series of ridges and grooves on the area between a calf's upper lip and nostril that is different from any other. What's more, these identifiers will grow larger as the animal ages, but the pattern of ridges and grooves remains the same.

C. E. Mace investigated many cases during his long career. In January 1932, he assembled evidence in the theft of twenty-seven head of cattle that resulted in the arrest of two people. Mace, assisted by Los Angeles and San Bernardino County sheriff's deputies, arrested Mary Messler and Al Hickam. They confessed to stealing cattle on the desert ranges of both counties.

In the spring of 1934, Inspector Mace was involved in what was publicized as one of the largest group of cattle rustlers in recent years.

Mace, along with San Bernardino County sheriff Ernest T. Shay and three deputies, arrested five men at Cactus Flat. During the raid on the rustlers' place, a hundred-gallon alcohol still and a truck full of army supplies stolen from March Field were found. The men admitted to stealing cattle from the Talmadge Brothers' Los Flores Ranch. One rustler made a statement to the judge: "Those steers had been hanging around our water supply and were muddying up our spring, and besides your honor, we were very hungry and in need of fresh meat." With the Depression well underway, the man probably spoke the truth. Two of the men were given probation, while the other three were held pending the army's criminal investigation.

The following year, Mace was involved in yet another case involving a quintet of rustlers. Four of the accused had been arrested while authorities searched for the fifth. Mace assisted in interviewing and securing confessions of the four men for stealing twelve head of cattle from the J. P. Loubet ranch near Chino. They had taken the cattle to the Los Angeles stockyards where they were paid $666 by check. Three months later, Inspector Mace and Los Angeles police lieutenant C. C. Mills arrested the fifth member of the group.

In August 1935, the *Los Angeles Times* sent a reporter to find out just what the state of affairs was regarding the rustler situation. There were over 350,000 head of cattle on ranges within a four-hour drive of Los Angeles, a city of 1.25 million in the mid-1930s. The sixteen rustling convictions in Los Angeles courts during the first seven months of 1935 served to illustrate the problem at hand.

The "rumble-seat rustlers" employed a technique of cutting a range fence and driving their car in late at night. They would drive slowly into the herd, grab and tie up calves, and deposit them in the rumble seat. They could usually fit four or five calves, which would net them about eight dollars apiece. Trucks were employed as well, allowing for a larger take.

Whereas rustlers of the Old West often stole cattle to enlarge their own herds, by the 1930s money was the primary incentive. Inspectors for California's cattle protection service were kept busy at all livestock markets and packing houses. The service also investigated theft cases and compiled evidence for prosecution.

The *Times* reporter rode with Deputy Sheriff Charlie Kelley, who was assigned strictly to policing rustlers due to his background in the cattle business. As they drove and visited with various ranchers, the deputy pointed out all the open range country that still survived, which made pickings easy for thieves. Deputy Kelley's beat, eighty miles long and twenty miles wide, contained mountains, forests, valleys, eight major ranches, gold camps, and saloons. He explained that the big ranches lost nearly $2,500 per year to rustlers. A major problem was that the courts often handed down suspended sentences to cattle thieves. They didn't take into consideration the great losses suffered by producers and filed them away as an "echo of the past." They completed the day's patrol of 140 miles, without covering the deputy's entire beat. The city reporter came away with a much deeper understanding of the cattlemen's problems with rustlers.

Yet again, *Popular Mechanics* published another article on cattle rustling. The October 1951 issue featured "The New West Still Fights Rustlers." The states of affairs in 1951 were covered in different areas of the country. An Idaho sheriff said, "The hunter who doesn't get his deer is our biggest cattle-rustling headache in these parts." In one case, the sheriff proved to be a bit of a Sherlock Holmes. He used a magnifying glass to examine a suspect's truck that had been thoroughly washed. He was still able to find blood and bone samples, along with blood samples from the suspect's boots. He was able to complete his case with an arrest when the FBI laboratory report came back confirming the samples were all bovine.

The article explained that during the previous winter, two men had slaughtered a heifer in a pasture where they found it and loaded the meat in their car. They started to drive away but got the car stuck in mud. They were unfortunate, as help arrived shortly afterwards in the form of a deputy sheriff. Idaho brand inspectors had checked over eight hundred thousand head of cattle in 1950, which involved five thousand different brands. Washington brand inspector C. F. Adams commented on how useless small brand designs were, because they usually ended up leaving a blurred mark. He recounted the arrest of two rustlers who were sentenced on four counts, to sixty years each in the Washington state penitentiary. Experienced brand inspectors are a valuable resource in fighting thefts.

One of these men was Utah inspector Alfred Martin, who had thirty-five years' experience in 1951. It was said that he could identify the owners of over eight hundred brands without referring to the state brand book.

Blaine County, Oklahoma, sheriff Raford Scott said that rustling was worse in 1951 than the previous sixteen years that he'd been a lawman. He related the story of one very hardworking rustler who would fill his truck with stolen cattle and drive three hundred miles away to sell them. Instead of driving all the way back with an empty truck, he would steal another truck load to sell back home.

The article also told of a rancher at Wood Lake, Nebraska, who lost 126 cows and 70 calves to rustlers in 1937. The next year they got thirty head more. The rancher was so angry that he bought an airplane to patrol his range.

When folks today hear about cattle rustling, it's more likely to have come from a John Wayne movie or a Louis L'Amour novel. It's a quaint Old West notion like stealing horses or drinking sarsaparilla from a dusty saloon at high noon. Livestock theft is not a hanging offense, but it is still a serious crime in the twenty-first century that continues to plague farmers and ranchers. The declining rural population appears to have made it easier for thieves. More and more family ranches have sold out to large operations and corporations. The network of neighbors who historically watched out for one another has been greatly reduced. In turn, it has become more of a problem for large operations to closely monitor their livestock, especially if kept on large tracts for grazing. Additionally, a period of time may elapse before missing stock is even discovered, which reduces the chances for recovery. Sometimes thefts go unreported because of pride and to avoid the appearance of vulnerability, or the belief that the chance of recovering the stock is very low. The following is a sampling of rustling cases and enforcement across the modern West.

In September 2001, a Phoenix, Arizona, man was arrested for seven felony counts involving livestock laws. Inspectors of the state agriculture department obtained evidence that the man had stolen more than 130 head of cattle, forged a proof of sale document, altered brands, and transported the cattle to Texas. The loss was estimated at over $100,000. In early 2016, a rancher near Willcox, Arizona, reported that fifty-four cows and their calves were taken from one of his pastures. The 108 head of livestock stolen was worth $162,000. Sadly, this wasn't the first theft the rancher had experienced.

The chief of the California Bureau of Livestock Identification reported in 2013 that cattle rustling was on the rise. He indicated that the previous year, 1,317 head of cattle were stolen or missing in California, which was a 22 percent increase from the year before. The laxity of the courts in taking cattle theft seriously is obvious, because felony charges are often plea-bargained down to a misdemeanor, with a fine and no jail time. When they are punished, probation is the usual sentence. A positive note, however, came when the governor signed a new bill that sets potential fines for stealing cattle. The new law took effect January 1, 2014, and calls for fines up to $5,000. The fines are paid to the Bureau of Livestock Identification instead of the state's general fund. During 2015, California bureau inspectors were involved in the recovery of thirty-two head of cattle and the arrests of fourteen people. Reports of the bureau indicate that in the last quarter of 2016, multiple cases were recorded that represented ninety-seven stolen or missing cattle. This did not include an undetermined number of calves involved in one case.

In 2014, Colorado Brand Commissioner Chris Whitney reported that the number of livestock reported missing or stolen almost tripled from 331 cases in 2010 to 829 in 2011. Morgan County had some serious thefts over the previous two years. A rancher reported that thirty-eight cows and forty-nine calves, worth $121,650, were stolen in 2012. Over the next year he reported the theft of forty-six cows and fifty-five calves, valued at $96,500. During the calendar year 2016, a total of 105 missing/stolen reports involving 537 head of livestock were filed in Colorado. The approximate value of the animals that went missing was $537,000. A few cases, however, do turn out simply to be livestock lost in remote summer pastures.

Blamed on soaring cattle prices, Idaho rustling increased in 2014. Brand inspector Larry Hayhurst said in December of that year that cattle worth about $350,000 went missing in southeastern Idaho. The cattle included a herd of fifty Black Angus, consisting of twenty-five cows and twenty-five calves worth about $150,000. A separate herd lost forty-one cow-calf pairs (eighty-two total), plus ten cow-calf pairs from another rancher were reported missing worth about $200,000. Earlier that year, the brand board arrested a man trying to sell ten dairy cattle from a dairy who didn't even know they were missing. The Idaho State Brand Board reported that the previous spring nineteen calves were suspected of being stolen. In February 2016, two men were arrested for stealing two cows and two calves from a cattle company. With calves valued at around $1,200 per head, they make appetizing targets for thieves. Also in 2016, two employees of an Idaho rancher were arrested for sixteen counts of grand theft following a rustling investigation. A routine brand inspection revealed that the two men had no proof of ownership for the cattle. The value of the cattle stolen between January 2015 and January 2016 was $19,200. Both men were jailed under a $50,000 bond each.

To address over $1 million in Kansas cattle losses between 2011 and 2014, a special crime unit under the agriculture department was formed. The unit consists of lead investigator Kendal Lothman, former Kiowa County sheriff, whose job it was to battle rustling in the Sunflower State. During 2014, reports show that fifty-six thefts occurred. These resulted in the loss of 225 head of cattle worth $330,264.

John Granger, administrator of the Montana Department of Livestock, Brands Enforcement Division, said that rustling is still alive and well, but quite often it's financial in nature. A man buys cattle and the seller finds that the check is worthless. He stated that in 2013, the department returned more than $6 million worth of cattle, horses, and sheep to their owners. Horses continue to be a prize for thieves, especially mares carrying a foal, like the one a family lost. The pregnant mare vanished—no carcass, no damaged fences, she was just gone. The financial loss was about $6,000. There is a genetic DNA code for the unbranded mare registered with the American Quarter Horse Association, but unless the thief tries to sell her and someone pulls a few hairs for testing, she is not likely to be found.

From 2009 through 2013, Nebraska Brand Committee (NBC) inspectors recovered, through ownership inspection, 9,066 head of cattle for 3,574 producers. Value of the stock was nearly $8 million. NBC criminal investigators effectuated fifteen felony and misdemeanor convictions that involved 412 head of cattle valued at over $338,000. From 2008 through 2012, the committee received 458 reports of violations of the Livestock Brand Act. Such violations included leaving the Brand Inspection Area without inspection, buying and selling cattle without brand inspection, use of an unrecorded Nebraska brand, no transportation permit, and failing to report an estray.

Sometimes the thief comes to the inspector. In November 2013, an individual from Ainsworth requested an NBC brand inspector to inspect cattle he had just acquired from a local feedlot. The bill of sale looked suspicious to the inspector, so he called the feedlot to verify. They had not sold any cattle to the suspect. The inspector called in the area NBC investigator and impounded the eleven head of cattle. The suspect was arrested for selling, trading, or disposing of livestock without a bill of sale, a Class III felony. He was sentenced on August 25, 2014, to 180 days in jail and three years' probation.

On July 15, 2014, Rebecca Robbins and Benjamin Johnson were arrested for stealing thirty-five cows and forty calves from a farm in

Nebraska state brand inspector Jason Gardner working at the Kearney Livestock Auction. AUTHOR'S PHOTO–COURTESY NEBRASKA BRAND COMMITTEE

Antelope County. A third suspect, Errik Dummitt, was arrested later. Robbins was convicted and sentenced to three to ten years at the York women's prison. Johnson was sentenced to sixty months' probation, 500 hours of community service, and ordered to pay $8,209.50 in restitution. The third suspect received twenty-four months' probation, 180 days in jail, court costs, and $600 restitution.

A ghastly livestock crime was reported in Nevada, in September 2014, and sadly it is still happening. The report indicated that twenty-six head of cattle were shot in the Martin Basin area. Five of these animals were killed outright, two were near death, and the rest had not been killed outright but were gut shot and suffered from horrific open abdominal wounds. By October fundraising for a reward fund was well underway by the Nevada Cattlemen's Association, Farm Bureau, Department of Agriculture, businesses, concerned citizens, and ranchers who had been affected by this crime over the past three years. The reward at the time was at $8,850 with an additional $10,365 for conviction of the person(s) responsible. As of 2017, the number of shot cattle rose to sixty-five, with ten dead and fifty-five walking wounded, including a three-month-old calf with most of its jaw shot off. The current reward offering of $26,200 is yet unclaimed. The Nevada Department of Agriculture Brand Inspection Division and sheriffs' offices in Lander, Humboldt, and Elko Counties continue to investigate these hideous crimes.

One of the more peculiar rustling cases in New Mexico occurred in April 2012. A Luna County deputy sheriff stopped three men in a Honda Civic. One of the men shared the back seat with a stolen 220-pound calf. The three went directly to jail and were charged with larceny of livestock, conspiracy, lack of a bill of sale, and exporting livestock.

North Dakota Stockmen's Association (NDSA) inspector Fred Frederikson said in a 2010 news interview that he investigates bank fraud, mail fraud, theft by deception, and, of course, good old-fashioned cattle rustling. One of those cases was a report of thirteen Black Angus cows and twelve calves missing in Burleigh County. Some of these cattle were found mixed in with a neighbor's herd, but others worth $24,000 were still missing. Some of the more unfortunate cases the inspector has worked involve abandoned horses: People who don't want the horses dump them off and they are found wandering around. Nelson County sheriff Kelly Janke was searching for missing cattle in 2011. He got close to what he was looking for, but when men brandished rifles, he wisely pulled back and called for assistance. The North Dakota State Patrol, a SWAT team, and deputies arrived, along with a Predator drone that was used to locate the men and cattle. The men were arrested and cattle returned to their owner. This was the first case where rustlers were caught with the help of a drone.

In 2016, the NDSA, and sheriffs of Morton and Sioux Counties had been investigating the wounding, killing, and theft of livestock. They confirmed that butchered cattle and bison were found in northern Sioux and southern Morton Counties. In a pasture where six animals were killed, a $3,000 registered blue roan horse had been killed and left mutilated. NDSA chief brand inspector Stan Misek stated, "The crimes against livestock in the area over the past several months have been appalling." A standing $14,000 reward existed for information leading to the arrest and conviction of any person(s) responsible. A November 2016 press release from John Hoeven, US senator from North Dakota, indicated that he and NDSA executive vice-president Julie Ellingson met with the US Department of Interior and the Army Corps of Engineers in Washington. Ellingson reported problems that ranchers were having with trespassing, vandalism, theft, fire, and roads being blocked by protestors of the Trans-Canada Pipeline Project. She went on to tell the officials about the butchered, mutilated, injured, and missing cattle, horses, and bison in areas adjacent to sites occupied by the protesters. Ellingson reported that livestock losses included one bull, two horses, three bison, four cows, thirty missing cows and calves, and two injured cows. The criminal investigations continue.

A former Lincoln County, Oklahoma, associate district judge turned himself in to Chandler authorities in 2013. He was charged with embezzling thousands of dollars from clients, harboring a fugitive, and—what else?—cattle theft. In February 2016, he was sentenced to five years in the state penitentiary and was ordered to pay $527,734 in restitution. The man had been an attorney for twenty years.

Jet McCoy of *The Amazing Race* fame lost one hundred cows to rustlers in 2014. Two suspects stole the cattle gradually, over time, until they were finally missed. Chief of the Oklahoma Department of Agriculture's Investigative Services Unit said that both suspects admitted to being users of methamphetamines. Both had a record of prior drug offenses. In 2015, agriculture investigators revealed that five people, ages sixteen to twenty-two, had been involved in a cattle rusting ring. Two had been arrested. Officials believe the group had stolen tens of thousands of dollars' worth of cattle, including a single sale for $27,000.

To step up penalties for cattle theft, the Oklahoma legislature passed a bill in 2016 that allows for a separate felony charge for each animal stolen. In the past, if twelve cattle were stolen, the suspect was charged with one felony. Jail time set for thieves remained at three to ten years, but those convicted could be fined three times the value of animals or machinery stolen.

Livestock officers from Oregon, Nevada, and Idaho have been plagued with cattle thefts in the Great Basin, which reaches into these states and Utah. This government range land provides excellent grazing for ranchers and the wide open places make cattle rustling easy. A 2010 news release indicated that ranchers started talking with one another and with law enforcement only to discover that around 1,200 cattle, with a value of $1 million, had been stolen. Ranchers began keeping a closer watch on their herds and even installed hidden cameras. A $60,000 reward was posted.

In October 2016, a fifty-five-year-old woman was convicted of cattle theft in Salem, Oregon. She pleaded guilty to committing theft of livestock valued at $10,000. The thefts took place between 2013 and 2014. She was ordered to pay $18,000 restitution and also paid a $200 fine for disfigurement of earmarks and obliterating brands.

A twenty-seven-year-old man pleaded guilty to stealing thirty-one calves from South Dakota ranchers in April 2015 and selling them on Craigslist. The man was sentenced to seven years in the state penitentiary for the theft of eleven calves from a Hyde County rancher. The case was one of the first investigated by the South Dakota Division of Criminal Investigation under an agreement with the state brand board.

Ronald Shepard, age thirty-six, violated a federally supervised release on bank fraud charges in March 2012 in Illinois and went missing. The US Marshals Service learned through their investigation that at least four states, including Texas, had, or were in the process of issuing, arrest warrants for livestock-related crimes. That May, while Shepard was still missing, a Rains County, Texas, grand jury indicted him on three counts of cattle theft. The Texas and Southwestern Cattle Raisers Association (TSCRA) special rangers were investigating the case and shared information with the marshals. Four months after Shepard had gone missing, US marshals located the wanted man in Mexico, and he was extradited back to the United States.

A cattle theft investigation by TSCRA special rangers that included DNA testing to confirm ownership prompted a Chireno man to turn himself in. The man was charged in 2014 with stealing at least eight head of cattle from two different neighbors.

In March 2014, TSCRA issued a news release that reported a major theft case. The Braum's Dairy Farms, on the Texas–Oklahoma border, near Follett, Texas, reported the theft of 1,121 head of Holstein/Jersey cross steer calves. Value of the calves was estimated to be $1.4 million. A $10,000 reward was posted.

The state of Utah has not been immune to the rise of cattle rustling in recent years. In 2015, a Carbon County ranch operation reported that they had more than two dozen calves go missing. They were trying to determine if they were lost or stolen. Another rancher reported the theft of five cows and over a dozen calves. The Carbon County sheriff's office estimated the loss at $31,000. Because of heavy rustling activity, the sheriff's offices in Carbon, Grand, and Emery Counties have formed a task force to fight cattle thieves. Various cattlemen's groups have donated thousands of dollars to the task force as reward monies. Tipsters are rewarded in cash for usable information.

Numbers released by the state indicated that from January to September 2014, 256 head of cattle were reported missing or stolen. During the same period in 2015, thefts of 144 horses and cattle, and 80 goats were reported. By May of 2016, the Utah Division of Animal Industry's fifty-five full- and part-time brand inspectors had begun new procedures in the fight against rustlers. Using fully marked vehicles, they spend more time patrolling and watching rural areas. They also distribute informational flyers to educate the public. Officials believe the new proactive approach has already made a difference in the number of thefts.

A Washington case began in 2011 when a dairy owner noticed some of his own cows going through the Toppenish Livestock Commission, the largest livestock auction in the state. Two men who had worked for the victim were jailed in late 2016 after more stolen cattle showed up in the sales ring. Washington brand inspectors are on hand for every auction at the Toppenish Livestock Commission. They can inspect upwards of two thousand animals on auction days. During 2015, over 700,000 livestock inspections were conducted there, with 1,800 being held for ownership verifications. The agriculture department's investigators worked eighteen cases of cattle and horse theft during 2015. In late 2016, Yakima County had one felony cattle theft pending. After the brands were blotted, the stolen cattle were transported to Oregon.

An increase in cattle theft was reported in Wyoming by mid-2014. Five cases were reported by June, where they usually only investigate a handful a year. High beef prices were suspected in the increased thefts. The *Wyoming Tribune Eagle* reported that a fifty-to-hundred-pound calf could sell for $375, compared to $100 in 2000. In August 2016, the Wyoming Livestock Board Law Enforcement and Investigations Division arrested a man for livestock rustling and misbranding or altering livestock brands. He was lodged in the Sublette County jail.

The modern rustling problem extends onto Indian reservations as well. A unique enforcement problem was discussed in mid-2015 regarding livestock thefts on the Wind River Indian Reservation. The Wyoming Legislature's joint House and Senate Agriculture, State and Public Lands, and Water Resources Committee met with representatives of the Eastern Shoshone and Northern Arapaho tribes and the Wyoming Livestock Board. In a nutshell, the problem of livestock law enforcement lay with jurisdictional problems. The livestock board has no jurisdiction on the reservation, and the Bureau of Indian Affairs (BIA) has no statutes regarding rustling and related livestock crimes. By December 2015, the

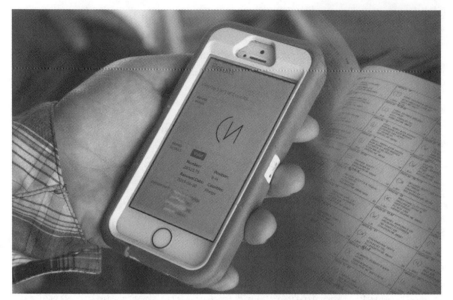

Modern technology allows an entire state brand book to be at the inspector's fingertips with a cell phone. The hard copies are still on hand, however. AUTHOR'S PHOTO–COURTESY NEBRASKA BRAND COMMITTEE

legislature's committee had sent a letter to the BIA encouraging them to establish a reservation livestock investigator.

Most state livestock agencies agree that the best protection for owners is branding, registration, and inspection. Unfortunately, branding isn't required in all states. Livestock producers have discussed a national identification system where cattle would be tattooed or computer chips implanted.

The International Livestock Identification Association (ILIA) is one such organization looking at cutting-edge technology to fight rustlers. Founded over seventy years ago, the ILIA is dedicated to the protection, promotion, and preservation of livestock and inspection in North America. The association rejects any animal activists who would have a negative effect on the livestock industry and has a mission to help educate the general public, along with local, state, provincial, and federal officials on the critical importance of the industry. One of the new technologies discussed at their 2016 conference was an ear chip that could be placed on a cow that would send a cell phone alert if the animal moved off the owner's property.

Another well-established organization is the Western States Livestock Investigators Association (WSLIA). The association has been around for over forty years and describes their mission as "To protect the livestock industry from theft, disease and harm, utilizing the latest technology and techniques with partners across state borders." Their members include law enforcement, state agricultural agencies, federal agencies, and private industry. The WSLIA is dedicated to continued training and information transfer to successfully investigate, apprehend, and punish perpetrators.

So, to answer the question "They don't rustle cattle anymore . . . do they?" some things change, but some, like rustling, have stayed the same, only the technology has changed. Just as rustlers have carried on into the twenty-first century, so have organized law-enforcement agencies who utilize the latest tools in combating them.

Bibliography

Books

Abbott, E. C. ("Teddy Blue"), and Helena Huntington Smith. *We Pointed Them North: Reflections of a Cowpuncher*. Norman: University of Oklahoma Press, 1971.

Alexander, Bob. *Fearless Dave Allison: Border Lawman*. Silver City, NM: High-Lonesome Books, 2003.

———. *Lawmen, Outlaws, and S.O.B.s: Gunfighters of the Old Southwest*. Silver City, NM: High-Lonesome Books, 2004.

Atherton, Lewis. *The Cattle Kings*. Bloomington: Indiana University Press, 1961.

Ball, Larry D. *Tom Horn: In Life and Legend*. Norman: University of Oklahoma Press, 2015.

Browning, James A. *Violence Was No Stranger: A Guide to the Grave Sites of Famous Westerners*. Stillwater, OK: Barbed Wire Press, 1993.

Burroughs, John Rolfe. *Guardians of the Grasslands: The First Hundred Years of the WSGA*. Cheyenne, WY: Pioneer Printing and Stationery, 1971.

Butcher, Solomon D. *Pioneer History of Custer County Nebraska*. Broken Bow, NE: Purcells, 1976.

Carlson, Chip. *Tom Horn—Killing Men Is My Specialty*. Cheyenne, WY: Beartooth Corral, 1991.

Chrisman, Harry E. *The Ladder of Rivers: The Story of I. P. (Print) Olive*. Denver, CO: Sage Books, 1962.

———. *Lost Trails of the Cimarron*. Denver, CO: Sage Books, 1961.

Clem, Alan L., and James Rumboltz. *Law Enforcement: The South Dakota Experience*. Watertown, SD: Interstate Publishing, 1982.

Collector, Stephen. *Law of the Range: Portraits of Old-Time Brand Inspectors*. Livingston, MT: Clark City Press, 1991.

Cook, J. H. *Fifty Years on the Old Frontier*. New Haven, CT: Yale University Press, 1923.

Cunningham, Eugene. *Triggernometry*. Caldwell, ID: Caxton Printers, 1934.

Cushman, Dan. *The Great North Trail*. New York: McGraw-Hill, 1966.

Davis, John D. *Wyoming Range War*. Norman: University of Oklahoma Press, 2010.

DeArment, Robert K. *Alias Frank Canton*. Norman: University of Oklahoma Press, 1996.

Dobie, J. Frank. *The Longhorns*. Boston: Little, Brown, 1941.

Drago, Harry Sinclair. *The Great Range Wars: Violence in the Grasslands.* New York: Dodd, Mead, 1970.

Frink, Maurice. *Cow Country Cavalcade: 80 Years of the Wyoming Stock Growers Association.* Boulder, CO: Johnson Publishing, 1954.

Forrest, Earle R. *Arizona's Dark and Bloody Ground.* Caldwell, ID: Caxton Printers, 1936.

Gard, Wayne. *Frontier Justice.* Norman: University of Oklahoma Press, 1949.

Gillette, James B. *Six Years with the Texas Rangers.* New Haven, CT: Yale University Press, 1963.

Goff, Richard, and Robert H. McCaffree. *Century in the Saddle.* Boulder, CO: Johnson Publishing, 1967.

Gresham, Hugh C. *The Story of Major David McKee: Founder of the Anti-Horse Thief Association.* Cheney, KS: Hugh Gresham, 1937.

Haley, J. Evetts. *Charles Goodnight: Cowman and Plainsman.* Norman: University of Oklahoma Press, 1949.

Harvie, Robert A. *Keeping the Peace: Police Reform in Montana 1889–1918.* Helena: Montana Historical Society, 1994.

Hendrickson, Robert. *Happy Trails: A Dictionary of Western Expressions.* New York: Facts on File, 1994.

Heritage of Clarks, Nebraska. Compiled and edited by the Clarks Bicentennial Heritage Committee, 1976.

History of Merrick County, vol. 2. Dallas: Taylor Publishing, 1967.

Hoy, Jim. *Riding Point: A Centennial History of the Kansas Livestock Association.* Fargo, ND: Institute for Regional Studies, 1994.

Hufsmith, George W. *The Wyoming Lynching of Cattle Kate 1889.* Glendo, WY: High Plains Press, 1993.

Hutton, Harold. *Doc Middleton: Life and Legends of the Notorious Plains Outlaw.* Chicago: Swallow Press, 1974.

———. *Vigilante Days: Frontier Justice Along the Niobrara.* Chicago: Swallow Press, 1978.

Idaho State Brand Book. 1936.

Jordan, Phillip D. *Frontier Law and Order.* Lincoln: University of Nebraska Press, 1970.

Jordan, Teresa. *Riding the White Horse Home.* New York: Pantheon Books, 1993.

Kelly, Charles. *The Outlaw Trail: The Story of Butch Cassidy and the "Wild Bunch."* New York: Bonanza Books, 1959.

Leakey, John. *The West That Was: From Texas to Montana.* Lincoln: Bison Books, 1965.

Lee, Bob, and Dick Williams. *Last Grass Frontier: The South Dakota Stock Grower Heritage.* Sturgis, SD: Black Hills Publishers, 1964.

Mercer, A. S. *The Banditti of the Plains.* Norman: University of Oklahoma Press, 1954.

Merrick County's 100th Year 1858–1958. Merrick Co. Nebraska Historical Commission, 1958.

Mortensen, Robert K. *In the Cause of Progress: A History of the New Mexico Cattle Growers Association.* NMCGA, 1979.

Nebraska Blue Book. Lincoln: Nebraska Legislative Council, Editions: 1915, 1922, 1924, 1940, 1972, 1994–95.

Nebraska State Brand Book. Editions 1943, 1994.

Nevada State Brand Book. 1961.

New Mexico State Brand Book. 1914.

New Mexico State Earmark and Brand Book. 1949.

O'Neal, Bill. *Encyclopedia of Western Gunfighters.* Norman: University of Oklahoma Press, 1979.

Osgood, Ernest Staples. *The Day of the Cattleman.* Minneapolis: University of Minnesota, 1929.

Pence, Mary Lou. *Boswell: The Story of a Frontier Lawman.* Cheyenne, WY: Pioneer Printing and Stationery, 1978.

Perkins, Doug, and Nancy Ward. *Brave Men and Cold Steel: A History of Range Detectives and Their Peacemakers.* Texas and Southwestern Cattle Raisers, 1984.

Prassel, Frank Richard. *The Western Peace Officer.* Norman: University of Oklahoma Press, 1972.

Preece, Harold. *Lone Star Man: Ira Aten, Last of the Old Texas Rangers.* New York: Hastings House, 1960.

Raine, William MacLeod. *Famous Sheriffs and Western Outlaws.* New York: New Home Library, 1944.

Respectfully Quoted. Washington, DC: US Government Printing Office, 1989.

Rollinson, John K. *Pony Trails in Wyoming: Hoofprints of a Cowboy and a U.S. Ranger.* Lincoln: University of Nebraska Press, 1941.

Sandoz, Mari. *The Cattlemen.* Lincoln: University of Nebraska Press, 1958.

Savage, I. O. *A History of Republic County Kansas.* Beloit, KS: Jones and Chubbic Art Printers, 1901.

Siringo, Charles A. *A Cowboy Detective.* Lincoln: University of Nebraska Press, 1988.

Smith, Helena Huntington. *The War on Powder River: The History of an Insurrection.* New York: McGraw-Hill, 1966.

Thrapp, Dan L. *Encyclopedia of Western Biography.* Spokane, WA: Arthur H. Clarke, 1988.

Vestal, Stanley. *Dodge City: Queen of the Cowtowns.* Lincoln: University of Nebraska Press, 1972.

Wellman, Paul. *The Trampling Herd.* New York: Cooper Square, 1974.

Webb, Walter Prescott. *The Great Plains.* New York: Ginn, 1931.

Yost, Nellie Snyder. *The Call of the Range.* Denver, CO: Sage Books, 1966.

———, ed. *Boss Cowman: The Reflections of Ed Lemmon 1857–1946.* Lincoln: University of Nebraska Press, 1969.

MAGAZINES

Aeschbacher, W. D. "Development of Cattle Raising in the Sandhills." *Nebraska History,* January–February 1947.

Bishop, Joan. "Vigorous Attempts to Prosecute: Pinkerton Men on Montana's Range, 1914." *Montana: The Magazine of Western History,* Spring 1980.

Blackburn, Dr. Bob L. "The Anti-Horse Thief Association." *Oklahombres,* 1997.

Canton, F. M. "The Wyoming Cattle War." *Cattleman,* March 1919.

Chapman, Dr. B. B. "Anti-Horse Thief Association Played Big Role in Territory." *The War Chief*, March 1974.

Chrisman, Harry E. "When Slow Elk Comes High." *Old West*, Summer 1965.

Cordry, Dee. "The Only Legal Hanging in Blaine County." *Oklahombres*, 1998.

Cosner, Sharon. "Branding Irons." *Americana*, July–August 1978.

DeArment, Robert K. "Wyoming Range Detectives." *Old West*, Fall 1993.

Devereaux, Jan "Gentle Woman, Tough Medicine." *National Association for Outlaw and Lawman History, Inc.* Quarterly April–June 2003.

Dobie, J. Frank. "Detectives of the Cattle Range." *Country Gentleman*, February 1927.

Frey, Phil. "Anti-Horse Thief Association Rounded 'em Up in Early Day Oklahoma." *Orbit*, February 1973.

Gass, Olive. "Vigilantes of Eastern Nebraska." *Nebraska History*, January–March 1933.

Gibbs, Rafe "The New West Still Fights Rustlers." *Popular Mechanics*, October 1951.

Hawthorne, Roger. "Conflict and Conspiracy." *True West*, June 1984.

Hewitt, Bob. "A Look at Brand Inspection in the West Part 1." *Western Horseman*, January 1972.

———. "A Look at Brand Inspection in the West Part 2." *Western Horseman*, February 1972.

Hope, B. W. "Joe Elliott's Story." *Annals of Wyoming*, Fall 1973.

Keen, Patrick. "The Anti-Horse Thief Association in Old Oklahoma." *Oklahombres*, Summer 1997.

Madden, Dennis, D. "The Hord Family: Merrick County Entrepreneurs." *Nebraska History*, Summer 1989.

Milek, Dorothy. "Killings in Wyoming." *True West*, January 1984.

The Nebraska Cattleman. July 1945, February 1949, July 1949, August 1949, September 1949, July 1957, October 1957, February 1958, March 1958, November 1965, March 1966, May 1988.

Nordyke, Lewis. "They're Still Rustling Cattle!" *True West*, January–February 1958.

Peterson, Marc. "Half an Inch of Dirt." *True West*, July–August 1958.

Potter, James E. "Thomas B. Hord: From Open Range to the Largest Live Stock Feeding Enterprise in the United States." *Nebraska History*, Fall 2015.

———. "Mike Shonsey." *Nebraska History*, Fall 2015.

Pollack, Jack. "Head Them Up." *Nebraskaland*, January 1967.

Rosse, J. C. "Nebraska Brands 1976—Brands A Valuable Property to Owner." *The Nebraska Sheriff*, May 1976.

Ryland, Lee. "Deep Ran the Blood in Buffalo." *True West*, January–February 1962.

Schuessler, Raymond. "A History of Cattle Rustling." *Cattleman*, October 1979.

"Trapping Modern Cattle Rustlers." *Popular Mechanics*. March 1939.

Trenholm, Virginia C. "Last of the Invaders." *True West*, January–February 1962.

Waldeck, Billy B. "Terror to the Rustlers." *True West*, November–December 1977.

Walker, Don D. "From Self-Reliance to Cooperation: The Early Development of the Cattle Associations in Utah." *Utah Historical Quarterly*, Summer 1967.

Ward, Nancy. "The Brand Inspector 1883–1983." *Cattleman*, July 1983.

"Where the West Is Still Wild." *Popular Mechanics*, November 1933.

NEWSPAPERS

Aberdeen Daily News (SD), April 25, 1929.

Aberdeen Times (SD), December 14, 1939.

AHTA Weekly, News February 20, March 6, 8, 13, May 29, June 12, 26, 1902; July 16, August 6, 20, September 10, 17, 24, 1903; October 19, 1905.

Alliance Times-Herald (NE), April 2, 1988.

Anaconda Standard (MT), December 17, 1890; May 25, 1902; June 16, 1903; September 26, 1904.

Arizona Daily Star, May 10, 1919.

Arizona Republic, October 10, 1944; February 14, 1950.

Arizona Weekly Star, October 19, 1882.

Atlanta Journal-Constitution, October 9, 1988.

Billings Gazette (MT), July 8, September 27, 1904; March 10, 1905; March 27, March 31, 1908; May 28, June 1, 1909.

Bisbee Daily Review (AZ), March 25, 1908.

Bismarck Daily Tribune (ND), October 11, 1905.

Bismarck Tribune (ND), April 14, June 12, 1997; November 17, 2010; October 15, 2016.

Black Hills Union and Western Stock Review (SD), May 14, 1909.

Blackfoot Morning News (MT), April 19, 2016.

Carbon County Journal (MT), May 27, 1892.

Central City Republican-Nonpareil (NE), August 1954.

Cheyenne Leader (WY), May 24, 25, 26, 1893.

Citizen-Republican (SD), March 31, 1910.

Clarks News (NE), August 12, 1954.

Coconino Sun (AZ), August 15, 1919.

Copper Era and Morenci Leader (AZ), July 9, 1915.

Daily Ardmoreite (OK), August 10, 1915.

Daily Capital (KS), October 21, 1879.

Daily Deadwood Pioneer-Times (SD), June 7, 1921.

Daily Independent (MT), August 6, 1897.

Daily Intermountain (MT), May 9, 1899, May 8, 1900.

Daily Missoulian (MT), November 12, 1912.

Daily Oklahoman, August 25, 1932.

Daily Yellowstone Journal (MT), January 10, June 23, 1885.

Dallas Weekly Herald, December 8, 1881.

Dawson County Herald (MT), June 20, 1988.

Denver Post, February 20, 1977.

Deseret News (UT), June 4, 2015; May 5, 2016.

East Oregonian, June 28, 1906.

Evening Times (ND), January 23, 1906.

Everest World (WA), September 22, 1966.

Fallon County Times (MT), May 17, 1926; May 15, 1939.

Fergus County Argus (MT), January 5, 1898; July 6, October 5, 1904.

Fergus County Democrat (MT), March 31, April 21, 1908.

Forest City Press (SD), August 15, 1912.

Fremont County Ranger (WY), June 7, December 20, 2015.

Gothenburg Times (NE), May 26, 1993.

Great Falls Daily Tribune (MT), December 22, 1920.

Great Falls Tribune (MT) July 17, 1886; April 20, July 3, 1904; January 26, 2015.

Hastings Tribune (NE), December 15, 2014.

Hot Springs Weekly Star (SD), June 29, 1894; July 6, 1894.

Idaho Daily Statesman, December 27, 1967.

Imperial Press (CA), April 27, May 11, 1901.

Kansas City Star (MO), February 17, 2015.

Kansas City Times (MO), October 6, 1937; September 13, 1949; September 22, 1961; November 15, 1962.

Kansas Farmer, June 6, 1883.

Lincoln Journal-Star (NE), August 7, 1954; December 12, 1973; June 7, 1992; December 2, 1997.

Los Angeles Times, August 18, October 11, 1935; January 5, 1936.

Mitchell Capital (SD), July 26, 1889.

New North-West (MT), January 22, 1897.

Newton Kansan, August 22, 1922.

North Forty News (CO), July 21, 2014.

Oasis (AZ), December 17, 1898.

Oklahoman, April 26, 2013.

Omaha World Herald, August 6, 1954; June 5, 1974; December 12, 1993.

Parsons Eclipse (KS), August 26, 1909.

Pierre Weekly Free Press (SD), December 16, 1909; April 7, 1910; July 13, 1911; December 7, 1911; May 8, November 13, 1913; December 13, December 27, 1917.

Pittsburgh Headlight (KS), May 19, 1958.

Police Collectors News (WI), April 1987, June 1989.

Post-Register (ID), April 14, 2016.

Provo Daily Herald (UT), May 5, 2016.

Rapid City Journal (SD), April 10, 2015.

Red Lodge Picket (MT), October 4, 1901; December 6, 1901.

Reuters, February 4, 2015.

River Press (MT), March 10, May 19, June 30, August 11, September 15, 1886; December 23, 1903; April 1, 1908; November 13, 1912.

Sacramento Bee (CA), October 27, 2013.

Saint Paul Globe (MN), July 3, 1904.

San Bernardino County Sun (CA), January 1, 1932; April 7, April 19, 1934.

Sand Springs Leader (OK), March 25, 1981.

Santa Fe Daily New Mexican, July 18, 1895.

Semiweekly Billings Gazette (MT), May 9, 1902; June 10, September 13, 1904.

Spokesman-Review (WA), April 24, 1979.

St. Louis Post-Dispatch, February 21, 1993.

Stillwater News-Press (OK), February 6, 1977.

Tombstone Epitaph (AZ), May 25, August 10, 1919.

Topeka Capital, March 19, October 8, October 19, October 20, 1911; April 6, August 9, October 22, 1915; March 25, October 19, 1917; November 23, 1918; December 21, 1924; October 29, 1937; June 13, 1938.

Turner County Herald (SD), December 3, 1908; December 8, 1910.

Valentine Democrat (NE), October 8, 1903; October 24, 1907.

Walla-Walla Union-Bulletin (WA), December 7, 1986.

Wichita Daily Eagle (KS), November 18, 1885.

Wichita Eagle (KS), November 26, 1937; September 9, 1969.

Wyoming Tribune Eagle, June 16, 2014.

Yakima Herald (WA), September 4, 2016.

Yellowstone Journal (MT), March 1, 1884.

Yellowstone Monitor (MT), March 26, 1908.

DOCUMENTS

Annual Report of the Cattle Sanitary Board of New Mexico, 1898–1900.

Anti-Horse Thief Association (Kansas Division) History, Objects and How to Organize, 1906.

Anti-Horse Thief Association Black List (Oklahoma Division), 1901.

Anti-Horse Thief Association (Oklahoma Division) Official Roster of Territorial Sub-Orders.

Anti-Horse Thief Association Proceedings of the Fifty-Fourth Annual Session of the National Order, Las Vegas, NM, 1916.

Arizona Livestock Board and Brand History, Arizona Department of Agriculture, 1990.

Bailey, Rebecca. "Wyoming Stock Inspectors and Detectives 1873–1890," thesis, University of Wyoming–Laramie, 1948.

Biennial Report of the Kansas State Brand Commissioner 1951, 1960.

Billey v. North Dakota Stockmen's Association, Civil No. 970332, June 4, 1998.

California Cattlemen's Association newsletter, 1998.

Cases Argued and Determined in the Supreme Court of Nebraska, January term 1881.

Collins, George. Personal archives.

Constitution of the State and Subordinate Orders of the Anti-Horse Thief Association by State Order AHTA of Kansas, 1892.

Drovers Cattle Network news release April 12, July 11, 2012; March 27, 2017.

Eastlake, Sandy. "Bunkhouse Business" newsletter of the Arizona Cattlemen's Association 1998.

Eisler, Gary. "History of the Oregon Cattlemen's Association" (manuscript) OCA.

Garvin Basin and Cattle Rustling. United States National Park Service-Big Horn Canyon National Recreation Area pamphlet.

Hoeven, Senator John (ND) news release, November 2, 2016.

Merimon, Larkin V. Written interview, February 14, 1938.

Montana Stockgrower 1884–1984, Montana Stockgrowers Association.

National Park Service, Garvin Basin and Cattle Rustling.

Nebraska Brand Committee, June 1945 map and information booklet.

Nebraska Brand Committee, news release, September 14, 2014.
Nebraska Cattlemen, Inc. newsletter, 1998.
Nevada Cattlemen's Association letter to author, December 2, 1998.
New Mexico Livestock Laws, Instructions to Inspectors, 1941.
Oklahoma State University, Some Ways to Identify Beef Cattle No. 612.
Records of Probate Court, Merrick County, Nebraska.
Records of the Wyoming Stock Growers Association.
Regulations of the New Mexico Sheep Sanitary Board, 1935.
Report of the Board of Stock Commissioners of Montana Territory to the Governor, 1884–1886.
Report of E. E. Clark for September and October 1923 to the Nebraska Stock Growers Association. Nebraska State Historical Society.
Second Annual Report of the Cattle Sanitary Board of the Territory of New Mexico, 1888.
South Dakota State Brand Board. "A Tale of the Hot Iron Brand," 1994 manuscript.
State of Idaho Legislative Services Internal Control Report State Brand Board, 1996.
Subordinate Order Ritual National Order of the Anti-Horse Thief Association, 1915.
Texas and Southwestern Cattle Raisers Association brief history, March 1992.
Texas and Southwestern Cattle Raisers Association news release, March 2, March 17, 2014.
Thorp, Russell. Personal accounting of Q&A with Mike Shonsey.
Transactions and reports of the Nebraska State Historical Society, 1887, 1893.
Washington Department of Agriculture Incident Reports, 2016.
Whitney, Chris. Colorado Brand Commissioner e-mail to author, February 3, 2017.
Wyoming Farm Bureau Federation news, August 5, 2016.

LAWS

Arizona Livestock Laws.
California Food and Agriculture Code, division 11, chapter 9.
Colorado Brand Laws Title 35.
Idaho Brand Laws Title 25, chapter 10, section 24-1010, chapter 11.
Kansas Session Laws 1939, 1943.
Kansas Livestock Brand Laws chapter 47, Article 4.
Montana Brand Laws Title 2, chapter 15, part 31.
Territory of Montana Laws, Resolutions and Memorials 1885.
Nebraska Revised Statutes chapter 54.
Nebraska Laws chapter 51, 1891, 1899; chapter 6, 1909; chapter 159, 1917.
Nevada Laws chapter 565.
New Mexico Brand Laws chapter 30, article 18; chapter 77, article 2.
New Mexico Brand Laws chapter 55, 1909.
New Mexico Cattle Sanitary Laws 1891.
North Dakota Brand Laws Title 36, chapter 36-09.
Oklahoma Brand Laws Title 2, chapter 1.
Oklahoma State Statutes Title 74, section 150.13.

Oregon Brand Laws Title 48, chapter 604.
South Dakota Codified Laws chapter 40, 1991, 1997.
Texas Brand Laws Title 6, chapter 144.
Texas Government Code, section 411.023.
Utah Brand Laws Title 4, chapter 24.
Washington Brand Laws Title 16, chapter 16.57; Title 43, 43.23.160.
Wyoming Brand Laws Title 11, chapter 20.
Wyoming Legislative Bill, Senate file SF0117.

WEBSITES
Beware, Not All Cattle Rustlers Are Men. www.cattlenetwork.com, July 11, 2014.
A Cattle Heist of Epic Proportions. www.texasmonthly.com, March 6, 2015.
Cattle Shootings Continue—Reward at $26,200. www.nevadacattlemen.org, January
    31, 2017.
Chireno Man Indicted on Three Counts of Cattle Theft. www.cattlenetwork.com,
    March 17, 2014.
Drone on the Range. www.prairiepublic.org, January 27, 2015.
Holt County Man Sentenced in Cattle Case. *Nebraska Brand Committee Bulletin.*
    https://nbc.nebraska.gov, January 21, 2017.
Hot Commodity: Reports Show Cattle Theft on the Rise in Some Places in U.S.
    Tri-State Livestock News. www.tsln.com, February 20, 2015.
John Smith Anderson. www.findagrave.com.
Livestock Group Eyes New Technology to Combat Cattle Theft. www.agweek.com/
    livestock, July 26, 2016.
Livestock Rustling Suspect Arrested. www.wyfb.org, August 5, 2016.
Marshals Nab U.S. Cattle Thief in Mexico. www.cattlenetwork.com, July 11, 2012.
Oklahoma Lawmakers Aim to Increase Cattle Rustling Penalties. www.cattlenetwork
    .com, April 13, 2016.
Ranchers Say Cattle-Rustling Risk High, but State Livestock Leaders Skeptical.
    http://dailyranger.com, June 7, 2015.
Samuel Neal "Sam" Moses. www.findagrave.com.
Stockgrowers, Sheriff Ask Help on Rustling from Reservation Tribes, State Legislators.
    https://dailyranger.com, December 20, 2015.
Three Thrifty Thieves. www.cattlenetwork.com, April 3, 2012.
TSCRA News Release: Authorities Seeking Information on Theft of Livestock at
    Braum's Farms. www.tscra.org, March 2, 2014.
Website bulletin. www.ndstockmen.org, January 21, February 23, 2017.

Index

About the Author

Monty McCord was given his first horse, a paint named Sally, at age seven. Growing up in rural Nebraska, he participated in many local 4-H horse shows. That soon evolved into Quarter Horse shows all over central Nebraska.

The author is a retired Hastings police lieutenant and graduate of the 174th session of the FBI National Academy at Quantico, Virginia. He writes fiction and nonfiction books about lawmen and outlaws from the Old West era to the mid-twentieth century. In 2013, McCord's *Mundy's Law* received a Peacemaker award for Best First Western Novel and was a finalist for Best Western Novel of 2013 from the Western Fictioneers, and a finalist in both the Will Rogers Medallion Awards and the Western Writers of the America Spur Awards. He lives in Nebraska with his wife, Ann.

Visit his website: www.montymccord.com.